# The Unnatural Aging of Cheese:

# From Partying to Parenthood

*To Sean & Theresa,
Please enjoy my pain!
Steven B...*

# The Unnatural Aging of Cheese:

# From Partying to Parenthood

a collection of humorous short stories

## Steve Chrisman

DANCING MOON PRESS
NEWPORT, OREGON

The Unnatural Aging of Cheese:
From Partying to Parenthood
copyright © 2011 by Steve Chrisman
All rights reserved

No part of this book may be used or reproduced, stored in or introduced into a retrieval system, or transmitted in any form or by any means (electronic or mechanical, photocopying, recording, or otherwise), without the prior written permission of the author, except in the case of brief quotations embedded in critical articles or reviews. Your support of the author's rights is appreciated. For permission, address your inquiry to Steve Chrisman through his website:
**www.schrisman.com**

ISBN: 978-1-892076-95-3
Library of Congress Control Number: 2011933999
Chrisman, Steve
The Unnatural Aging of Cheese: From Partying to Parenthood
1. Title; 2. Short stories; 3. Humor; 4. Humor: Marriage & Family;
5. Family Life;

*Author photo:* Shannon Chrisman
*Book design:* Carla Perry, Dancing Moon Press
*Original cover art:* Ed Cameron
*Cover design & production:* Jana Westhusign, StudioBlue West
Manufactured in the United States of America

DANCING MOON PRESS
P.O. Box 832, Newport, OR 97365
info@dancingmoonpress.com
www.dancingmoonpress.com
541-574-7708

FIRST EDITION

# Foreword/Dedication

Where was Ritalin when I was a kid? Until my late twenties, as an undiagnosed ADHD sufferer, I never found a problem, regardless of its size, that couldn't fit under a standard bathroom throw rug. And I certainly never did today what could be put off until tomorrow. Not surprisingly, things usually went horribly wrong by the time Monday arrived or I sobered up. Had my New Jersey high school(s) taken a poll of "Most likely NOT to succeed," or even survive, I surely would have ranked high—or low— depending on your perspective. My youth was spent being told, "You just need to apply yourself." God only knows how much more damage I would have caused had I done so.

Life is full of experiences and lessons; sometimes they're humiliating, sometimes painful. This is a collection of short stories, hopefully funny ones, of some of those humiliating and painful moments. It spans my early blossoming into a party animal, which got me kicked out of an expensive boarding school and flunked me out of two colleges, to my exile across the country to Oregon and my eventual migration up through

Washington and into Alaska, where I married my college sweetheart. It covers my not-so-meteoric rise to the top of middle management and the difficulties encountered raising two young girls, two dogs and two cats in a small, one-bath home on the Oregon Coast with a wife who may just be the worst cook on the planet.

You know, my life seems like an endless series of tests, but true to form, I've managed to maintain a C-average throughout. If you are married to a world-class underachiever, admit to being one yourself, or are struggling to raise one, then this book may give you hope. It might also scare the shit out of you. Whichever it is, please enjoy my pain. It's been a long climb to the middle, but I finally made it! After all, success is relative. Really.

One of the first things you notice about New Jersey is that everyone, rich or poor, jock or stoner, nerd or Neanderthal, has a nickname. Furthermore, you don't get to choose that name; it somehow chooses you. I'd love to say that I came to be known as "The Cheese" because I was a great leader among my peers, or possibly saved a puppy from an overturned pot of molten fondue, but it wasn't quite that glamorous.

In actuality, I was sent away to boarding school at the age of fourteen and all freshman football players were forced to write their name on a piece of masking tape and stick it to the front of their helmets so the coaches would know who they were. My last name is Chrisman, but Mr. Picariello, the tight ends coach, couldn't pronounce the "r" in Chrisman. Thus, I was called "Chis-man" (Chiz-man) for the entire two-week camp. My teammates latched onto that mispronunciation, dropped the "man," and started calling me, "Chizzer," and then, "Chiz" and then, "The Chiz" and eventually it worked its way into, "The Cheese" or just plain "Cheese."

Like I said, you don't get to choose, and regardless of how unusual or unflattering your name might be, you must accept it, proudly, like some misshapen badge of honor. It's a good thing by Jersey standards, akin to the English bestowing the title "Sir" on those chosen to be knighted.

Therefore, I'm dedicating this book to all those friends I grew up with, who still carry their nicknames proudly: Don Juan, De-vo, Pumpkinhead, Crazy Al and Doo, Grape Ape, House, Ippy, Jutdog, Turk, Magoo, Meatloaf, Meathead, Moondog, Pappa, Schmales, Boz, Weed, Flounder, Lumpy and Sludge, just to name a few.

Heartfelt thanks for the unwavering support of my mother-in-law, Terry, and my wife, Shannon, without whom this book would never have been published.

*Steve Chrisman*

# The Unnatural Aging of Cheese:

# From Partying to Parenthood

# Contents

Generation X-mas .................................................................... 1
A Tale of Two Hotrods ........................................................... 10
Banished Down the Oregon Trail ........................................ 19
Just for the Halibut ................................................................ 27
Jacques Peugeot ..................................................................... 51
The Short Arm of the Law .................................................... 64
Funeral Traditions ................................................................. 70
Toss the Meat .......................................................................... 78
The Pampered Pooch ............................................................. 82
Trash Day: The Need to Belong ........................................... 87
The Dousing of Mr. Dingles ................................................. 92
A Brush with Death ............................................................. 101
Black Friday: Operation Shop and Awe .......................... 108
You Can't Pick Your Sister ................................................. 116
McVooDoo .............................................................................. 121
Marital Issue #5: Poor Vehicular Hygiene ....................... 125
The Spice of Life ................................................................... 130
The Stowaway ....................................................................... 134
Sobe—So Bad! ....................................................................... 140
Why, You Cheating Dog, You! ........................................... 147
The Finch Who Stole Christmas ....................................... 152
If I Could Be Like Mike ....................................................... 162
About the Author ................................................................. 167

# Generation X-mas

**The 1980s were a self-indulgent time,** but, in hindsight, drinking up our Christmas tree money may have been a bit of a mistake on my part. It's hard to believe I was the first teenager to ever sink so low, but you sure don't hear about it much. I've always hoped it was just an under-reported statistic. Regardless, teenagers make mistakes, and in all fairness to me, my thirteen-year-old sister did take half the money. Well … not exactly *half*, but I gave her a substantial portion, relative to her younger age and inability to show any verifiable need.

In our defense, our father was a card-toting tightwad of the highest order. All airline pilots are cheap, but our father was the Ebenezer Scrooge of penny-pinching pilots. We had even nicknamed his wallet "Phil," because—like the famed groundhog—it had a tendency to peek out of his pocket, get spooked by its own shadow, and disappear for another six weeks. Thus, sightings of Dad's wallet, like that of Bigfoot and the infamous Jersey Devil, were rare and tended not to be believed.

# The Unnatural Aging of Cheese

Not so coincidentally, the old man seemed to always be away from home, flying over any holiday that involved gift giving, namely birthdays and Christmas. During the first ten years after our parents' divorce, we came to expect his pre-holiday exodus, however, when he asked us to forego getting a tree my senior year in high school, *well now*, that was just sinking to an all-new Scrooge-ian low.

Being cheap is one thing, but the thought of a tree-less Christmas was just too much. Our outrage must have shown, too, because he coaxed ol' Phil out in record time, slapped down $75 on the counter, and said he'd be back on the 26th of December. Feeling as if we'd just saved Christmas, we breathed a sigh of relief. Unfortunately, our sense of moral superiority was somewhat short-lived. There are certain crossroads we all come to in life that say a lot about who we are, and ... well ... let's just say that his exhaust cloud hadn't fully dissipated from the driveway before Sis and I had divvied up that dough.

We had a real good time with Dad out of the picture but four days passed much quicker than expected and before we knew it, December 26 had arrived. By that point, the idea of purchasing a tree and the money with which to do so were both just distant memories. On the day after Christmas, like most days, Sis came bounding cheerfully down the steps and that's when she spotted it—that glaring empty spot—where, in years past, a twinkling pine had once stood.

"Oh God," she stated matter-of-factly. "He's going to kill us."

## Generation X-Mas

The Jersey Shore isn't like Oregon, where you can run out your back door, cut down a tree, and drag it back inside. Jersey has laws. And even if I'd known where to find a forest, I didn't know anyone who owned a saw.

"Whatta we gonna do?" she asked.

"Find a tree," I said.

"Yeah, but where?" she asked.

A quick survey from the kitchen window revealed only one pine and, sadly, it was firmly planted in our neighbor's yard. After thirty minutes of sawing, we realized two things: one—that tree wasn't going to be felled; and two—our father had purchased the cheapest set of steak knives ever made.

As we sat around lamenting our situation, there came an unexpected knock at the back door. It sent chills up our spines.

"Oh, no! He's home!" Sis cried.

We'd thought we had until afternoon, but clearly our moment of atonement had arrived early. Being God-fearing red-blooded American teenagers, we did the only logical thing.

It was cramped in the coat closet with the two of us wedged in there, but it was conveniently located, and everyone knows there's safety in numbers. It took a minute, but it dawned on us that he wouldn't be knocking at his own back door. Warily peering around the door jam, we were relieved to discover it was just Mo—our ex-stepmother—our father's second ex-wife—and still our trusted friend and confidante. If anyone could save us, it was good ol' Mo. Sure enough, a couple minutes later she had a plan.

## The Unnatural Aging of Cheese

Her plan, so to speak, was to drive around the affluent shore town of Spring Lake, New Jersey, until we found someone who'd thrown out their tree early.

"That's the dumbest plan I ever heard," I told her. "No one throws their tree out the day after Christmas."

This was a practice, she assured me, of the upper crust, to prevent needles from dropping on their expensive carpets.

"Come on?" I said dubiously.

"It's true!" she said.

"Yeah, sure it is," I countered, "and if we're lucky, maybe they'll leave it fully decorated."

"Okay, Smart Man," she said, "then what's your plan?"

I took a moment to explain my plan, but once she pointed out that runaway shelters rarely if ever admitted boat-shoe-wearing preppies, I pulled the door shut on her '82 Saab hatchback and we headed out in search of a tree.

Two hours later, under overcast skies, we'd been up and down nearly every street in the town of Spring Lake, and all the Jersey pines were either deeply entrenched in someone's yard, or mocking us from inside the living rooms of less dysfunctional families.

"I knew this was a stupid idea," I said. It was pointless to continue, and even the eternal optimist, Mo, realized it was time to turn back. In a cowardly last-ditch effort to save myself, I asked her to stop by the Marine recruiter's office on our way home.

We had just turned in that direction when Mo yelled, "Hey, what's that!"

"Quit joking," I said.

"Yeah, it's not funny," Sis complained.

"No seriously," Mo said, "I saw something flash in the mirror."

Afraid of being duped, but hopelessly desperate, we turned to look.

I'm not sure how a man of science would explain what happened next, but logic would dictate that the hand of God reached down, parted the skies, and sent a beam of life-giving sunlight hurtling towards earth, where it glinted off a single vestige of tinsel that dangled ever-so tenuously from a branch of what had to be the only abandoned Christmas tree in the northern hemisphere, or certainly the Central Jersey Shore. It called to us, like a lonely castaway wielding a shard of mirror. As a light ocean breeze made the tinsel dance, we sat mesmerized, suffused in the heavenly glow from its intermittent flashes. There is occasion in one's life where you can just feel providence at work, and this was one such occasion.

With the tree of life now located, there remained the small problem of actually extricating it from the home-owner's yard without being noticed. It wasn't going to be easy though. Not only did she sit out in plain sight, but the ground cover was light and the street was lined bumper-to-bumper with the vehicles of holiday visitors. We made two passes to reconnoiter the situation, assess troop strength, and try to identify any weaknesses in their perimeter. On the third pass, fearing that some other pair of irresponsible teenagers might steal it before us, the passenger doors of the

# The Unnatural Aging of Cheese

Saab kicked open. Sis and I rolled out onto the asphalt, and *Operation Tree Snatch* was underway.

Mo went off to double-park as Sis and I scrambled between two bumpers and took cover with our backs against a couple trees. Craning my head, I peered in the picture window and counted nine guards in the mess hall, varying in age from eight to eighty. A less seasoned soldier could have easily mistaken them for an extended family. They were cleverly disguised in civilian garb, but their argyle sweaters and bright, shoulder-padded dresses were clearly mid-80s Army-issued suburban camouflage. And their barracks, with its four-story Victorian façade, wasn't fooling anyone.

From the looks of it, we hadn't been spotted yet.

Back in the car, we had worked out a highly complex system of verbal and non-verbal commands, so when I yelled, "Run, Dummy, run!" Sis knew exactly what to do. She took off after that tree as if our lives depended on it, which we were quite sure they did.

Sis was never what you'd call athletic, always leaning a little towards the big-boned side, but on that day she was a fleet-footed gazelle and it was all I could do to keep up with her. As if we had been born to steal trees off strangers' lawns, we reached that fallen pine, instinctively took our positions on either end, bent and lifted, and then we beat feet like the devil himself was on our trail. I don't remember—before or after—ever being that proud of her again. Why, if we hadn't been racing across a stranger's lawn, carrying a stolen Christmas tree, I probably would have stopped and hugged her right there.

## Generation X-Mas

Things couldn't have been going any better when we heard the unmistakable sound of clawed feet scrabbling across a wood-planked veranda, followed shortly thereafter by ferocious barking, vicious growls, and the gnashing of slobber-laden jaws. *Uh, oh*, I thought, *we've been spotted*.

We could hear them gaining on us as we approached the street, but frighteningly, our escape vehicle was nowhere to be seen. Seemingly out of nowhere, the Saab backed into view and skidded to a stop with its hatchback already raised. Scrambling in first, I crawled up into the passenger seat and looped my arm around the tree. Once I saw Sis crawl in, her face beaming with a sense of salvation, I turned around and yelled, "HIT IT, MO!"

We were at the end of the block when we realized Sis was no longer with us.

Just a cautionary note in case you ever find yourself riding in the back of a rapidly accelerating Saab, sitting next to a stolen Christmas tree with the hatchback up—apparently Saabs don't have much in the way of handholds. I assured Mo that Sis knew her way home and that she'd be fine, but Mo insisted on going back and kicked the car into reverse. Just as she was about to be overtaken, Sis dove in the back—again—and we sped off a second time, leaving that pack of snarling Pomeranians in our wake. Fortunately, their short little legs were no match for the sporty Swedish Saab.

Skidding into the driveway, we wrestled the tree into our house. Once inside, I immediately headed down to the basement for a stand while Mo and Sis shot to the attic for decorations.

# The Unnatural Aging of Cheese

"Go, go, go!" yelled Mo, "We don't have much time!"

As we rendezvoused back in the living room, we were greeted by the terrifying sound of the automatic door of our detached garage being activated. Some less efficient families will drag out that whole tree decorating process for days or even weeks, but not us. In the seven minutes it took our father to exit his vehicle, grab his bags, and walk down the cement path between the garage and the house, we erected a tree, strung three sets of lights, hung dozens of ornaments, and draped a prodigious amount of tinsel. At the risk of sounding boastful, another minute or two and we probably could have had that tree flocked. Admittedly, Sis setting up the Nativity scene was an unnecessary risk, but a nice touch all the same.

As the back door clanged shut, we were frantically shoving empty boxes under the couch. We hardly had time for a high-five before hearing him say, "Merry Christmas! I'm home!"

Dabbing sweat beads from our foreheads, we cheerily chorused, "Merry Christmas, Father!"

You can believe what you will, but Sis and I know we were led to that tree by some higher power ... like the three wise men. Only we weren't so wise, and our journey's purpose was somewhat less than holy, and we weren't on camels, and we bore no gifts—but similar all the same.

Well, there was no stable or hay, and no donkeys, and we weren't all men, but much the rest was very similar.

Actually, come to think of it, it wasn't really that similar, but still, we were led to that tree ... *somehow ... by something.*

## Generation X-Mas

We celebrated a belated Christmas that day, exchanging our customary one gift each, and I have to say, that was one of the most blessed Christmases we ever spent together. The three of us formed a pact and swore never to tell Dad what we'd done. To this day, he still doesn't know. And what he doesn't know can't hurt him. Or, more importantly, us.

# A Tale of Two Hotrods

**If only my old man had put a 1984 red BMW** in our driveway on my sixteenth birthday—like I was fully expecting—all my problems might have been prevented.

Instead, I found a rusted-out, 1974 Mercury Montego, which had to be the largest two-door car ever built. In place of my BMW's big shiny ribbon, there was a strip of silver duct tape holding the Montego's vinyl roof together. And worst of all, I didn't even get the pink slip—Dad just granted me the great honor of driving that motorized monstrosity.

According to the old man, the '74 Montego was a state-of-the-art vehicle when she came out, and she *was* loaded with bells and whistles. Unfortunately, most of them had stopped dinging and tooting long before I got behind the wheel. For example, the power antenna was perpetually stuck at half-mast, and by 1984 the eight-track tape player had become little more than a place to store my empty wallet. The power windows worked—on the way down anyways—but once they hit bottom, they would dislodge and fall into the doorframe. This wasn't so bad in the ninety-five-degree New Jersey summers, especially since the air conditioning was inoperable, but in the twenty-degree winters it got pretty unpleasant. Taking off the door panels was a big job, so I just scotch-taped a note on the window, warning the passenger not to touch.

The sun had burned almost all the paint off the car's hood, but if you squinted real hard it sort of looked like a Pontiac Firebird symbol. In fact, the sun had damaged so many spots along her exterior that she resembled a rolling Rorschach test. As far as the ladies went, I might as well have been cruising in a can of sexual tear gas. With bald tires and no suspension to speak of, she rode about six inches off the ground, which may have made me the unintentional inventor of the low rider. Night driving was a spectacle because she'd routinely bottom out and send off a rooster tail of sparks.

I'm not sure what passed for a bell and whistle in 1974, but the self-removing muffler seemed really impractical. It would fall off about once a week, and after my father would order me to go find it, I'd be forced to crawl underneath and reattach it. For some reason, the pipe coming out of the muffler and the one running under the car were about two inches short of connecting. My father had seen some car show where they cut a soup can lengthwise and used it to bridge the gap, so between 1984 and 1987, it's safe to say that Campbell's saw a sharp spike in their soup sales along the Central Jersey Shore.

In late August 1987, while en route to an end-of-summer blowout, I drove over the little Manasquan Bridge and the Montego got three flat tires all at the same time. "Come on," I said to myself, "what kind of luck is that?"

Since I was already running late and my divorced airline pilot father was away on a trip, I did what any responsible, eighteen-year-old high school graduate would do—I pulled into a real estate office and abandoned the car.

To be honest, I didn't really think much about it, until my father returned home three weeks later and asked where she was.

"At a friend's house," I lied. "I'll go get it."

To my great surprise, the real estate office didn't think it was good for business to have a rusted-out heap in front of their building.

Now, my old man is a very frugal guy, so he wasn't nearly as upset about my lie as he was about the $10 he had to pay for each day the car had been impounded, and the cost of the three new tires. When he said to follow him straight home, I just kept my mouth shut and *I followed*. Always a fast driver, he'd gotten a pretty good lead on me when the black, acrid smoke started billowing out from under my hood. Quickly, turning into a gas station, I hopped out, popped the hood, and upon seeing the flames, I did what any sensible person would do.

As I ran around the building to take cover from the imminent explosion, I heard what sounded like my father's voice far off in the distance. Peering out, I saw him racing back towards the station, with his head and arm out the window, flailing away and screaming something I couldn't

## A Tale of Two Hotrods

understand. As he pulled in, I realized he was shouting, "You *idiot*, put that out!" with a generous sprinkling of expletives. Well, I don't know what my father was watching back in the '80s, but on *Miami Vice* and the *A Team*, anytime a car catches fire, that car blows up. So I was very reluctant to follow his instructions. Three times he threatened my life before I finally grabbed a soapy bucket off the island, window squeegee and all, and threw it on those flames.

I'd be the first to admit that my father's a pretty smart guy, and he was right, those flames did go out, just like he said they would. In some respects, you might say we saved the gas station and its patrons that day, but from the looks of all the melted wiring, the same couldn't be said for the Montego. The old man wasn't about to pay for a tow truck, so as I learned the true meaning of the term *"if looks could kill,"* he tied an old rope around our bumpers. For a moment I thought about asking if his little European sports car should be used as a tow truck, but I didn't want to upset him any further. Fortunately, it was a convertible, so he just set that shiny bumper in the seat next to him, retied the rope to the frame, and we headed off for home.

Over the next few days Dad and I worked hard on repairing that car, but as it turned out, neither of us was mechanically inclined. In the end, it was a good thing the old man had purchased those three new tires, because the tow truck company charges less if they can just *drag* your car to the dump. Surprisingly, Dad wasn't as happy about the savings as I'd thought he'd be.

My old man was a real penny pincher, so watching the

# The Unnatural Aging of Cheese

Montego get towed away on three brand new tires, after he'd just paid for three weeks of impound, did not sit well with him. Survival over the next twenty-four hours was a bit touch and go, but the moment I felt sure he wasn't about to choke the life out of me with his own two hands, I felt compelled to share with him a new problem that had arisen—community college was starting the following Monday and I now had no transportation to get there.

"I guess you'll be riding a bike," he said matter-of-factly.

"That would take hours," I informed him, "and I don't think they let you ride bikes on the Garden State Parkway."

"Tough shit!" he said, still harboring just a bit of hostility.

In all honesty, I wasn't real keen on going to community college anyways, but I knew the old man thought education was his best bet to get rid of me, and if there was one thing my father feared beyond all else, it was the thought of me living with him for one moment more than New Jersey law required.

"Well," I said, feigning disappointment, "I guess I could just stay home and start next semester."

As the terrifying thought of us growing old together took hold in his mind, all he could say was, "No, no, no, no! I'll think of something."

And sure enough, true to form, a half-hour later the old man had hatched a plan. His pilot buddy, Darryl, lived in the Florida Keys but flew out of New York City. Between trips, Darryl would stay at our house on the Jersey Shore where he left a spare set of keys for a car he kept at the airport. Since I hardly knew the guy, I felt a little odd about

## A Tale of Two Hotrods

taking his car without permission, but the old man assured me Darryl wouldn't mind. "Why, we'll just use it until we find another solution and then we'll put it right back. What could possibly happen?" he asked, rhetorically.

Fathers know best, and since I was still on borrowed time, I just climbed in his car and we headed off for New York City.

Boy, oh, boy, and I thought my Mercury Montego was a piece of shit. I felt bad for complaining about it because Darryl's car was a canary yellow 1973 Chevrolet station wagon. Unbelievably, it was actually larger than the Montego, less attractive, and shared the same tread-less tires. Clearly Darryl and my father had been cut from the same cheap cloth. If I was having a hard time picking up chicks in the Montego, I could just forget about it in that eyesore. Having always been self-conscious, just the thought of arriving for my first day of college in that big yellow boat was making me ill. I stood there, wide-eyed, staring in stunned silence.

"Beggars can't be choosers," my father said, coldly. "Get in!"

That big beast did get me to college that first day and I may not have been able to pick up any chicks in her, but it sure didn't stop me from looking—which is probably why I was so slow to react to the brake lights in front of me. I was preoccupied with the hot blonde in the rearview mirror when suddenly I heard the sound of screeching tires. By the time I reacted, everything was in slow motion. I slammed my foot down on the brake, but Darryl's pedal went all the

## The Unnatural Aging of Cheese

way to the floor and by the time the brakes did start to catch, Darryl's tread-less tires might as well have been ice skates on a frozen pond. Finally, after about a week, that big boat came to a stop, thanks in great part to the car in front of me with the freshly crumpled trunk. When the middle-aged woman got out yelling and holding her neck, I knew I was in trouble.

"Hello—Darryl?" I said sheepishly. "Yeah, this is Gary's son, Steve ... Gary *Chrisman* ... Your *friend* ... from *New Jersey*? ... Yeah, well, I know you hardly know me, but uh ... my car burned up a week ago ... Yeah, thanks, I was sorry it happened too, but that's not why I'm calling exactly ... Uh, well, the reason I'm calling is ... uh ... my dad thought it would be okay if I borrowed your car, Darryl ... No, I'm not calling to ask permission exactly ... I sort of already borrowed it ... Yeah, really ... Oh, I didn't realize your insurance didn't cover other drivers. That's not good 'cause ... uh ... I ... had a little accident. Darryl? Darryl? You still there?" (Long pause) "Yeah, no, take a minute ... No, not real bad, but the police came ... No, I'm fine, but she was ... uh ... complaining about neck pain ... *boy*, I'm *really* sorry, Darryl ... No, please, take all the time you like ...." (Another long pause) "Yes, your car is *fine* ... It's got a little dent in the grill is all, but she drove like nothing happened ... You should see the other lady's car, though! ... No, I wasn't trying to be funny, I just meant ... comparatively speaking ... ah, *never mind*! I'm *so sorry, Darryl!* ... Absolutely, yes, I'll keep you updated."

After hanging up from the worst call I'd ever had to make in my short life, I asked my father how I was going to get to college now, and he said, "What do you mean? You just told Darryl his car was running fine."

"Yeah," I said, "but I don't think he really wants *me* driving it."

"Well, I don't really want *you* dropping out of college and living with *me* till you're 40, so *you'll* be driving it again."

"Okay, if you say so!" I said.

And so the next morning I returned for my second day of community college.

Day Two had gone pretty smoothly, but as I raced down the Garden State Parkway heading for home, the cloud of white smoke that appeared in the rearview mirror seemed strangely familiar. At first I assumed, because of its age, that Darryl's car just let off a little bigger cloud of exhaust than most cars. It wasn't until I slowed down some that I realized it was coming from under the hood. Since it wasn't as dark as the smoke from my earlier car fire, I naturally assumed the lighter colored smoke was a good sign. And since I was almost home, I decided to see if the old girl couldn't just ride it out. As we sailed over the next rise, from the general direction of the engine, there came a most unnatural cacophony of clinks and pings, and I immediately realized that we weren't going to be making it home. In a disturbing episode of déjà vu, I pulled over to the shoulder, hopped out and popped the hood.

"Oh, no," I said, "Not *again!*"

There was a tollbooth about a quarter mile up ahead, and as I took off on foot, I wondered what the odds were of

## The Unnatural Aging of Cheese

a person having two cars catch fire in one month. *Not good*, I thought.

As I was already somewhat of an expert on dousing car fires, I had hoped the toll booth operator would just hand me a fire extinguisher or a bucket of water, but as soon as I told him my car was on fire, he immediately grabbed for his phone. Maybe I was being self-conscious, but I thought one small fire truck would have been sufficient. The additional two trucks, the ambulance, and the three police cars seemed excessive. Fortunately, I managed to get my books out of the passenger seat before the foam bath began. If there is a humiliation greater than standing next to a burning yellow 1973 Chevrolet station wagon, holding your community college textbooks under your arm, alongside the Garden State Parkway at rush hour, I have not experienced it. The fact that there was an entire fire department, half a police station and 100,000 rush hour commuters there to share the experience was really just icing on the cake.

The cops gave me a ride to the nearest exit, where I called my father: "Dad, you're not going to believe this."

I hadn't been home more than ten minutes when he handed me the phone. "Uh, hi ... Darryl? Yeah, this is Steve again. Gary's son. Uh, the reason I'm calling is ... uh ...."

# Banished Down the Oregon Trail

**Most pioneers came willingly** down the Oregon Trail, but me—I was shoved. Banished, if you will, from my beloved Jersey Shore by a paternal dictator who had grown weary of my partying ways.

In the dark of night he had me carried off and whisked away west—to Oregon—with hopes that I would never be heard from again. And thus, like Napoléon before me, sans the grandiose ambitions—sans any ambitions, really—I was unceremoniously exiled. Oregon had become my Island of Elba. However, as was the case for Napoléon, that evil dictator had not seen the last of me. No, sir, I would return and he would rue the day he'd sent me away, because, as it turned out, I wanted no part of Oregon and Oregon wanted no part of me.

My grandfather generously left each grandchild a trust fund with which to attend college. Astonishingly, my father had never felt me worthy—something to do with my getting kicked out of an expensive boarding school a few years earlier—so he agreed to pay *only* if I could prove myself at

## The Unnatural Aging of Cheese

junior college first. I was a bit snobby then, and my friends had all gone to the finest schools in the country, so I was less than enthusiastic about attending a junior college in Jersey, which may explain why I failed to record a single credit in two full years of pretending to be attending. Now, as you know, my father is a very frugal man, so watching his only son flush two years of tuition down the toilet was difficult for him to stomach. So difficult, in fact, that, as nonsensical as it sounds, he agreed to pay for a four-year college out-of-state where I could waste tuition without his having to watch any longer. And thus, my inherent and seemingly effortless ability to underachieve had gotten me my way—again.

As a world-class partier, I quickly identified Arizona, southern California, and Florida as my destinations of choice. However—for the purpose of spying—the evil overlord agreed to pay for college only in a state where we had a high concentration of relatives. The old man had tricked me, but, left with a choice between rural Nebraska, where my redneck relatives had no running water, and rural Oregon, where at least they relieved themselves indoors, I quickly chose the lesser of two evils—Oregon it was.

As the son of an airline pilot, I had always enjoyed free passes and had visited southern Oregon many times. Now, from a northeastern suburbanite's perspective, southern Oregon—and more specifically Medford and Grants Pass— were like going back in time to roughly Prohibition era Appalachia. Those towns were the kind of places where a Yankee like me would just instinctively clench his butt

## Banished Down the Oregon Trail

cheeks and listen closely for the sound of banjos. That being the case, all good rats need to know when to abandon ship, and my free-ride father was beginning to list heavily to one side. To my great surprise, Oregon State University (in Corvallis) and the University of Oregon (in Eugene) did not accept students who graduated high school with a 1.69 GPA, so I was forced to scurry out the first open porthole I found.

*Where in the hell is Ashland, Oregon?* I remember thinking.

Boarding the plane at Newark International, I waved farewell to my beloved Jersey and made a silent vow to return someday. Admittedly, Ashland was a bit cuter than expected, but it was a complete mystery to me why they would have built two towns ten miles apart and left all that empty space in the middle. I felt quite sure I would die of boredom, but armed only with my thick Jersey accent and an insatiable urge to party, I did what I did best at the time: I made friends and I partied. And I partied. And I partied.

The first month of college was actually easier than I'd expected, due in part to the fact that I hadn't attended a single class. I'm not sure if I broke any records by drinking up an entire year's tuition, gaining forty pounds, and getting kicked out of college in thirty-one days, but it felt like I should have received some kind of formal recognition. For the record—I merely implied I would kill the dormitory attendant who confiscated the five cases of beer I had so inconspicuously carried through the front door.

It surprised me, on that thirty-first day, when the dean of housing asked me to pack my things and to please never

## The Unnatural Aging of Cheese

return. I'll be honest, I was a little shocked and a little hurt, but I know when I'm not wanted, so one month after arriving I sold back my nearly untouched textbooks—at fifty cents on the dollar—pulled out my free airline pass and boarded a plane, making a silent vow to return to Oregon someday soon. The Red Eye out of San Francisco allowed me plenty of time to think about how best to tell my father what had happened. Unfortunately, none of my lies sounded truthful enough, and after some deep deliberation, I decided it would be best for him not to know. After all, we weren't terribly close, and we almost never called each other, so by my calculations, it might be a year or two before he actually figured out I was no longer in Oregon. The only problem with that plan was that my father would kill me if he saw me, so I had to avoid detection.

Thanks in great part to Dad's excessive drinking, I was able to stay out all night partying, and then once he passed out in his recliner, I'd come sneaking in the house, through the kitchen, and past his snoring body in the TV room. Once by the gatekeeper, I'd alternate between going down to a storage room in the basement and up to an unused bedroom on the third floor.

This surreptitious existence was facilitated by the fact that my father was divorced, and although my grandmother had come to stay with him (from Oregon), she and my younger sister both went to bed early. In fact, my biggest challenge was getting past our dog, which was solved by stashing a cheap box of dog biscuits in a bush out back. So, while my father dreamt alcohol-induced dreams of an all-

## Banished Down the Oregon Trail

American son across the country, earning straight A's in college, the real fruit of his loins was tip-toeing past the top of his snoring head, a mere ten feet away.

It wasn't an ideal existence, but life was pretty good for a while. I managed to pilfer a throw pillow and an old afghan off the couch, and I even felt bold enough to start stealing leftovers out of the fridge. However, after three weeks of living invisibly, it began to take its toll, mentally and physically.

Sleeping in an oversized storage closet isn't as glamorous as it sounds, and I began to develop an awful kink in my neck. And some days I would be trapped for hours waiting for all of them to leave the house.

Eventually, I just couldn't take it any longer and so I decided it was time to come clean—but not to my father—that would have been suicide. No, I thought my grandmother would provide a much more sympathetic ear. So one morning, after over-hearing the old man say he was leaving on a trip, I snuck down to the second floor and awaited his departure. Standing at the window of our guest room, where my grandmother slept, I watched patiently as his car backed out of the garage and headed down the driveway. *Finally*, I thought, *this charade is about to end*.

The blood-curdling scream was so loud and unexpected that I nearly soiled my only clean pair of underwear. Crying out myself, I whipped around to see my terrified grandmother backpedaling out the doorway with one hand over her mouth, one over her heart, and a set of eyes the size of dinner plates. I had known she'd be upset, but clearly she

## The Unnatural Aging of Cheese

was overreacting. It was as if she didn't even know me. And that's when it occurred to me that the intruder standing before her had not shaved in weeks and weighed roughly 40 pounds more than her beloved grandson who was supposed to be attending college some three thousand miles away.

Performing mouth-to-mouth on your own grandmother takes a little getting used to, but once she started breathing again, why heck, she looked good as new, and I wasted no time in confessing the whole big mess. She sat wide-eyed as I recounted the entire tale and how I'd been living for the previous three weeks. And when I was done, I made her swear that she wouldn't tell my father. I'm not sure if all grandmothers are liars, or if it was just mine, but the old man hadn't gotten three feet in the door before she ratted me out. To my great surprise, he told me not to let the door hit me on my ass on the way out. And at that point, I became the first homeless man in history to wear a pastel polo shirt, khakis and boat shoes.

The first couple hours of homelessness weren't so bad, but it gets cold in New Jersey in November, and as it turns out, there's a severe shortage of homeless shelters in upper-middle class neighborhoods. Luckily, Don, my only friend not at college, came and got me and was kind enough to rent me the two-foot gap between his bed and the wall.

It wasn't the Four Seasons, but it was much better than a cement-floored storage closet. Unfortunately, once Don's mom realized I was living there, she very politely asked me to leave as well. A few days later, the police picked me up for being an intoxicated preppie vagrant, and they promptly returned me home again. Despite my father's emphatic insistence that he did not want me back, the cops insisted he keep me.

The next morning, at 0800 hours, Dad and I arrived at the Marine recruiter's office, where my father personally introduced me. I'd like to say that I was excited to join the Marines, but some of us just aren't cut out for military service. My fears were short-lived, because as luck would have it, I was too fat to join. Who knew? Apparently, if there's no war to fight, they didn't need fat cannon fodder like me. I tried not to chuckle, but man oh man was my father *pissed*. However, he's never been one to take no for an answer and so he just marched me down the hall. The Air Force told him that I was too fat to "aim high," and then the Army assured him that they did want men "to be all they could be," but that I was already a little too much. And lastly, the Navy said I could "see the world in the Navy" if I could see my way to losing about fifty pounds. We hit every branch of service except the Salvation Army, and each one told him I was of absolutely no value, which is why he was offering me to them in the first place.

On the way home, my father laid out an intensive workout plan for me to get back into football shape. One week in, I didn't even need to weigh myself; I knew I'd gained at least five pounds. And after seven months of watching me slowly put on weight, he begrudgingly threw in the towel on the whole military idea.

Now, every man has his breaking point, and since Dad

## The Unnatural Aging of Cheese

couldn't kick me out, couldn't ship me out, and—despite the look in his eyes—couldn't bring himself to kill me, he agreed to give me another shot at college. *If*, and only *if*, I was willing to leave *immediately*, a full two months prior to the start of school.

"Done!" I said.

The next day Dad drove me to JFK Airport where we exchanged a lukewarm handshake, and back out to Oregon I went, keeping my vow to return in the process.

Unbeknownst to him, I used the two months to lose forty pounds and I arrived back at school looking like I'd just gotten out of boot camp. So fit, in fact, that I attracted the attention of a beautiful and shy nineteen-year-old girl from Alaska. She provided a much-needed mellowing effect, and four years later I graduated. Okay, five years later, but who's counting.

# Just for the Halibut

"**Y**OU GODDAMN—MOTHER FUCKIN'—WHORE MONGERIN'—BUCK-TOOTHED—COCK SUCKIN'—SON-OF-A-BITCH!" shouted the gray-haired old man on the boat up ahead.

Seeing my pace slow down, my future mother-in-law, Terry, said, "Oh, don't mind that... That's just Doc. My daughter did warn you about him, didn't she?"

"Well, yeah," I said, "but she just said the man was a bit temperamental. Does he have Turret's or something?"

"No, that's just Doc," Terry said, "and, uh—he probably only pricked his finger right there, so you'd better get used to that."

*Good Lord*, I thought, *three days on a boat with this guy—what have I gotten myself into*?

Back in Oregon, I would sit in my college dorm and listen, mesmerized, as my future wife recounted tales of her life growing up on a secluded island in Southeast Alaska in the middle of America's largest national forest. Having been raised in New Jersey, the most populated state per square mile, I had a hard time fathoming that someone could live in such a place as she described—driving down the same twelve miles of paved road and staring at the same two thousand faces her entire life. I became enamored with the mere thought of this mythical place, so when my future mother-in-law and her husband invited me commercial halibut fishing, I literally jumped at the opportunity.

By the sheer grace of God, the halibut opening crossed right over my college Spring Break, so I scraped together every penny I had and bought a roundtrip ticket to Wrangell, Alaska, with stops in Portland, Seattle and the island city of Ketchikan, home to the now-infamous Bridge to Nowhere pork project.

I should have known I was in trouble when fog grounded my plane in Ketchikan. And in an act that could never have occurred on the uber-efficient East Coast, some dummy had built the airport on an *uninhabited island*, and another dummy I knew didn't have five dollars cash to take the cash-only ferry across to town. Luckily, panhandling proved easier than expected. However, I lost a quarter of my deckhand share by missing the boat prep stage of the trip. As my plane took off the next morning, I couldn't help thinking they could really use a bridge in that town.

My future mother-in-law, who is Scandinavian, Aleut Indian, and Russian, met me in the one-room, aluminum-sided airport. "Welcome to Alaska!" she said.

"Thanks," I said, "It's just how I pictured it."

She and I made small talk, waiting by the stainless steel baggage claim chute. To my great delight, a red light began to flash over the chute and then a human hand reached through the black curtain and slid the first bag down.

"As you can see, we're pretty high tech around here," she said.

"Yeah," I responded, "that's a real marvel of modern technology," and we laughed the whole five-minute ride to town.

I've always appreciated a good character, and let's just say there will never be another Doc. A *true* general practitioner, Doc was one of two town doctors, serving as both surgeon and self-taught obstetrician. He moonlighted as the town vet and classic car mechanic, and in his spare time, he commercially fished on his 54-foot steel-bottomed boat, the *Zimovia*.

When Doc turned to greet me he resembled a gift shop carving of a bearded fisherman right down to the pipe, with only the yellow slickers missing. His slickers were green. And his surly, dry-drunk demeanor could have only resulted from a reckless one-night stand between Captain Ahab and Blackbeard the Pirate. In his mid-to-late fifties, Doc stood roughly six feet tall and had a wiry frame. And although I outweighed him by at least sixty pounds, I felt quite sure he could kick my ass on sheer determination alone.

"You're late!" he barked. And that was how my first Alaskan adventure began.

"Ever been on a boat this size?" he asked.

"Sure," I said, surprising him, "but I think it was a bit bigger, actually."

## The Unnatural Aging of Cheese

"Really?" he said, making no attempt at all to mask his incredulousness, "Whadidit fish fer?"

"Jersey Blue Fish...I think," I replied.

"Ya think?" he said, suspiciously, "How is it you don't know?"

"Well," I said, "I was just on a summer booze cruise to see the Statue of Liberty."

"Aw, Jesus!" Doc hissed, shaking his head in disgust, "Talk about a fuckin' *greenhorn!*" After running off another award-winning string of expletives, Doc said, "All right, follow me."

*Man,* I thought, *this isn't starting out quite like I expected.*

Suffice it to say, Universal Studios won't be hiring Doc to give tours, but he did give brief landlubber explanations of the ship's many working parts and even pointed out a few hazards to avoid. "See this?" he said, pointing to a big metal pulley hanging just above his head.

"Yeah," I said.

"Don't hit your skull on this," he said, "it's heavy, split ya right to the bone."

"I'll be careful," I said, "I wouldn't want you to have to run me to a hospital."

"Hospital!" he exclaimed. "There won't be any hospital. I'd be stitchin' you up right here."

"Seriously?" I said, "You have Novocain on board?"

"NOVOCAIN!" Doc cried. "Jesus, yarn't a pussy, are you, son?"

I wasn't sure if I was more shocked by the question or by hearing a doctor use that term, but I was just about to tell him where to stick it, Jersey Style, when I heard myself squeak, "Uhhh … no, sir."

"Good," Doc said, "cause you'd be an awful big pussy if you were one."

Realizing that we hadn't even left the dock yet, I thought, *Oh, Lord, this trip is really gonna SUCK*.

Doc made a point to remind me that while I was laid up in Ketchikan, my crewmates had been doing *my* job. He led me to an overflowing barrel of cubed bait, and after telling me twice how long it took them to cut it, he said I was going to have the honor of baiting all the skates myself, which probably would have upset me more had I known what a skate was.

As Doc demonstrated shortly thereafter, commercial halibut fishing is done with a process called longlining. The fisherman lays out miles of what looks like mountain climbing rope across the ocean floor. Every six feet along the rope there's a much smaller gauge rope, called a gangion, that's about three feet long with a four-inch metal hook on the end. Each section of the eight miles of mountain climbing rope gets rolled into two-foot conical stacks, called skates, with the hooks hanging on the outside. There appeared to be unbaited skates covering much of the dock and most of the boat's stern. It was my job to put two-by-two-inch hunks of semi-frozen salmon on each hook.

"We set sail at dark," Doc snarled, "so you better get baitin'."

My new crewmates sat in the wheelhouse watching me flounder, and they let me finish about ten skates before coming out to help. Our four-man crew included Doc, my future mother-in-law Terry, me, and a fifty-something salty dog named Paul who spent most of the year teaching school in Tacoma, Washington, but spent his summers fishing Southeast Alaska.

As a seasoned veteran, Paul held the honored position of fish-cleaner. Seeing him pull out what must have been a thirty pound salmon and begin cubing it for more bait, I made the mistake of asking why we were baiting the hooks with salmon, which I presumed to be a much more expensive fish. They all looked at each other and laughed.

"Boy, that's dog salmon there," Doc said. "And it ain't fit for the dogs. Nobody eats Dog Salmon," he warned, "'cept maybe you Easterners."

*Man*, I thought, *I'm getting the distinct feeling this guy doesn't like me.*

When we finished baiting the skates, Doc gave me a two-minute lesson about how, one at a time, I was going to stack each skate into a three-foot tall chute at the back of the boat, where it would uncoil at a very fast pace. And when it started getting close to the end, I was to attach the end to the next skate and move *it* into the chute, and so on and so forth until we'd laid out the whole eight miles of rope. *Seemed simple enough*, I thought.

"Oh," Doc said, "one more thing. There's no stoppin' 'em and those hooks whip out fast, so stay clear, understand?"

"Sure," I said jokingly, "I don't want to get stitched up with no Novocain."

## Just for the Halibut

"Forget stitches," Doc snapped, "You get hooked and you'll go straight to the bottom. Lucky for you, you'll drown before getting there, but then I'd be mailing you back to New Jersey, and from the size of you, I don't want to pay that kind of postage."

As Paul and I untied the mooring lines, I thought, *Dear Lord, please don't let me die out here in the middle of nowhere with this crazy pirate who hates me.*

Boats are like wives to a fisherman, and the *Zimovia* was Doc's second boat but his first love. And if you count his first three ex-wives, and my mother-in-law, then that makes ... well, it gets confusing.

Anyways, after I made the near unforgivable faux pas of questioning the boat's sea-worthiness, Doc assured me that her steel construction made her nearly unsinkable. He said that my falling overboard was actually a much more likely scenario, and with the temp of the water, I'd probably live only fifteen minutes, which wasn't nearly enough time for him to stop the boat and get me.

*Oh, good,* I thought, *that's comforting.*

The sun was close to setting as we steamed off for the open waters of the Pacific. As I looked back at the electric glow of tiny Wrangell, I took a moment to take in my surroundings and was overcome by the vastness and seclusion of Southeast Alaska. Seventeen million acres of temperate rain forest is nearly incomprehensible for most Easterners — for most anyone really. Uninhabited islands, carved from the last ice age, jutted up in every direction, with vegetation so lush it seemed to leave no space uncovered. Gloriously

## The Unnatural Aging of Cheese

absent of people, there was an abundance of all other life that one would have thought would be found only in a tropical jungle. Western hemlock and Sitka spruce, hundreds of feet high and hundreds of years old, grew right down to the water's edge, sometimes hanging out over the sea at seemingly impossible angles. Southeast Alaska is not seen, it's experienced, and I had never experienced anything remotely like it. As Wrangell disappeared behind a promontory, so too did any reminders of the modern world. It was like we had traveled back in time to a period before people, to a simpler time where only shelter and sustenance and survival really mattered. I thought about just how far from the hustle and bustle of New Jersey I'd come, and, for the first time since I'd arrived, felt something other than fear, frustration, and loathing.

"Hey, Boy, get up to the bow and check the waterline," Doc shouted.

I had just finished swabbing the deck and could only imagine what horrible task lay in store.

"You see it?" he shouted over the roar of the engine.

"See what?" I shouted back.

"The glow, Boy, the glow!" he yelled.

*What is this crazy old man talking about now?* I thought, but that's when I saw it ... *What in God's name?*

At the turbulent water's edge, where the bow cut through, the water was glowing the most unnatural fluorescent blue-green I'd ever seen. Like a true Jersey Boy, I shouted, "What is it? Pollution?"

"Naw, it's no *God-damned* pollution!" Doc screamed.

## Just for the Halibut

"It's bio-luminescent plankton that's excited by the boat's bow. Ain't it something?"

*Yeah,* I thought, beautiful—spectacular, really. And to think, until that moment, I hadn't even known such things existed.

While I was gazing into the glow, something suddenly darted by just beneath the surface. It was so unexpected that it caused me to recoil. *Jesus, what in the hell was that?* I thought. It was incredibly fast and appeared to be four or five feet long with dark coloration. And then another shot by ... and another ... and another. There must have been eight or ten of them down there.

"We've just been joined by a school of Dall porpoises," Doc shouted through the wheelhouse window. "They can reach thirty knots and they love ships. It's like a game for 'em. Watch! They'll probably escort us out to the Pacific."

Sure enough, for the next hour, I watched as they jetted back and forth, changing speeds and angles, occasionally leaping and seemingly trying to outdo one another. I found myself wishing my friends and family could see what I was seeing. Did they know this world existed? How had I not known it existed? *If the trip ended right then,* I thought, *or we didn't catch a single fish, this would have still been worth it.*

And then it was dark. And dark in Alaska is a whole different level of dark from New Jersey. There is no artificial light ... anywhere. No endless string of coastal towns with millions of houses and streetlights to help orient a wayward captain. No, on an overcast night, Alaska achieves true pitch black, save the eerie green illumination of the wheelhouse sonar and the blue-green glow of the plankton below. For all intents and purposes, the world I'd known before had been blotted out entirely, and it was only faith that allowed me to believe it was still out there ... somewhere. Maybe it was just the Jersey Boy in me, but staring out into the vast empty darkness, I thought, *You know, there's something incredibly serene about this level of sensory deprivation.*

During dinner I was treated to many tales of past fishing excursions, and even more tales of Doc's excessive, larger-than-life exploits. He was really quite an amazing man. Like a walking Greek tragedy, Doc's life was one long list of astounding over-achievements followed closely by mind-boggling falls from grace.

Born to a poor fishing family in Depoe Bay, Oregon, Doc was blessed with a photographic memory that allowed him to rise above his humble beginnings. At eighteen, he had joined the Marines, where they quickly recognized the boy's potential, moving him into Officer Training School and allowing him to graduate college four years later. Doc never talked about it, but Paul whispered that as a young lieutenant, Doc backed a truck into a minefield and saved a couple of injured soldiers. And he'd probably have won a medal of some sort if it hadn't been *his* dereliction of duty that allowed them to get in that predicament in the first place. Thus, in the end, his commanding officer agreed to just not court marshal him.

Next, Doc paid his own way through med school at the University of San Francisco, and when I met him, he'd been sober three years, after losing his license to practice for a year.

## Just for the Halibut

Doc was a legendary binge drinker who had reportedly been drinking while on call. However, the locals, almost to a man, would happily tell you they'd rather go to Doc stinkin' drunk than to any of them Lower-48 docs sober. He was their kind of doctor—a rough, tough, straight shootin' son-of-bitch who fit their blue-collar fishing community just perfect. He let the poor folk go long periods without paying, and would sometimes accept fish and venison as compensation. He delivered a good majority of the children born in that town over the previous twenty years, and most of the locals felt deeply indebted to him.

All that aside, Doc was still one surly sour son-of-a-bitch, but for reasons you couldn't quite explain, you sorta couldn't help but like him. His abhorrent bedside manner was a thing of legend. And if you were unlucky enough to be in his waiting room when he was treating a pregnant sixteen-year-old or a cheating fisherman with a case of the clap, then you'd undoubtedly overhear Doc's own special brand of expletive-laced life counseling and preventative medicine. And God forbid you were a logger who got busted up in a bar fight at two in the morning, because he was gonna make you wait 'til he finished his beer, and you could just forget about any Novocain for making him drive into town. But then that was Doc, take him or leave him, love him or hate him. He made no apologies and he asked for no sympathies. You knew what you were gonna get. Had he endangered his patients' lives? Quite possibly. How many lives had he saved over the previous two decades? Quite a few.

# The Unnatural Aging of Cheese

Doc was a great man who carried a great many demons inside. Though gifted both mentally and physically, he never seemed to think himself worthy of those gifts or of anyone's love. That inner turmoil manifested itself in angry outbursts, in railing against God and man and all their creations. By the time I met him, he had three ex-wives and four estranged children, and a few years later, after fourteen years of not-so-blissful marriage, my mother-in-law would make it a fourth ex-wife with a fifth to come. Oddly enough, Doc was fair and just with everyone except those closest to him. For them he made himself nearly impossible to love long-term. It was really quite sad.

Doc said we'd be sailing through the night to reach the fishing grounds by morning. He suggested we get some shut-eye because the twenty-four-hour halibut opening would start at noon sharp and there would be no sleeping after that. For the uninitiated, a twenty-four-hour opening is just as it sounds: Each boat has exactly twenty-four hours straight, noon to noon, to catch as much halibut as possible. Any fish pulled after noon of the second day would need to be thrown back or you'd risk losing your license and your boat. This is deadly serious business to the fishermen of Alaska.

As a college student and a seasoned veteran of the all-night kegger party, I figured staying up twenty-four hours was going to be a snap. Boy was I in for a big surprise.

In his least gruff tone, Doc said, "You, fellas, better hit the hay. We have a big day tomorrow."

Paul and I climbed down into the engine room, which

sat adjacent to our sleeping quarters. While I grabbed a top bunk, Paul pulled the hatch shut to drown out some of the deafening engine noise.

"Well," Paul said, "what do you think so far?"

"It's been interesting," I said. "The scenery has been spectacular, but I'm not sure what to make of old Doc just yet. I think he hates me."

"Naaaah," Paul said, "that's just how Doc is first time you meet him." Then on second thought he added, "Actually all times you meet him, but he don't mean nothing by it. S'long as you work hard, you'll be fine."

"If you say so," I said. "Good night, Paul."

"Good night, Mary-Ellen," he replied.

"Fuck you, Paul," I said.

"Fuck you, Mary-Ellen," he responded.

Between the excitement of the coming day, the roar of the engine, and the smell of diesel fumes, sleep did not come easy. Regardless, Doc woke us six o'clock sharp, and after a hearty breakfast we were out on deck prepping for the big start. Noon came up fast and I stood at the ready by my three-foot metal chute, among an endless number of baited skates. The whistle blew and the race was on. Fortunately, the weather was very good by Southeast Alaskan standards, so all I had to do was concentrate on my one job. The first ten hours were spent laying down the line in two long strands across the ocean floor, the logic being that you don't place all your luck in just one spot, and by the time you lay down the second strand, it's time to pick up the first. Doc wasn't kidding when he said those hooks come

## The Unnatural Aging of Cheese

whipping out, and each time one went whipping by me I got a very vivid image of myself being dragged to the ocean floor. I tried not to dwell on it, but the thought of being halibut bait was never far from my mind.

We took a quick dinner break at 10:30 p.m., during which my crewmates reminisced about past halibut openings. To my great disappointment they let slip that halibut fishing had never been Doc's specialty. In fact, he'd had only one really good season in the past sixteen, which was a little discouraging since I'd just spent every penny I had to get there. I felt like an 1850 gold miner who'd just made a harrowing journey into the wilderness, only to hear the gold rush was over.

Around eleven o'clock, Doc popped up from the dinner table and announced it was time to pull the first line.

It took an hour to get back to the start of the first line. As you might imagine, locating a little orange buoy in the pitch-black in the middle of the Pacific Ocean is even harder than it sounds. Doc had asked me and Paul to go up on the bow and keep a lookout because he thought we were getting close. Sure enough, a minute later, Paul yelled out that he'd spotted it, and after returning to the stern, he hooked the buoy line as it floated by.

This was it. You could just feel the atmosphere on the boat change. We were all nervous but excited to see what results our hard efforts would reap. Doc told me to stand by his side as he ran the line through the winch and pulley. He informed me that I would now have two jobs: One was to recoil each segment of rope as it came back up from the ocean floor and the second was to stand at the ready in case we landed any really big halibut. Having never seen anything bigger than a thirty-pound dog salmon, I couldn't help wondering how big these fish got. Embarrassingly, it occurred to me then that I had no idea what a halibut looked like, but Doc didn't need any more fuel, so I just kept that fact to myself.

I am quite confident that my fellow landlubbers have no idea what sorts of nasty beasties dwell at the bottom of the ocean, and if they did, then they'd probably never step foot in the water again. In that first hour, we caught just about everything the ocean floor had to offer—*except* a halibut. There were mini-sharks called dogfish and mini-rays called skates. There were the heavily fanged and prehistoric-looking lingcod and the florescent orange red snapper with its hideously bulging eyes and its depressurized fish bladder jutting through its open mouth like an enormous red tongue. Skate after skate, gangion after gangion, arrived at the water's surface with something other than a halibut.

At first Doc used this as a biology lesson, pointing out each species and their distinguishing features, but he quickly reverted to a string of expletive-laden tirades about how f-ing unlucky we were. I began to worry I might have needed my fish gaff less to land a big halibut than to defend myself from Doc's building rage.

Just before the bulging veins in Doc's neck and temples burst, he shouted, "FISH ON!" meaning we actually had a halibut coming to the surface. The crew breathed an audible sigh of relief, but our relief was short-lived.

# The Unnatural Aging of Cheese

"GOD—DAMNED—SAND—FLEAS!" Doc screamed, staring at our first halibut dangling in the air. It had probably been a sixty-pounder; however, it was now missing all its flesh save the head and tail and a small strip down one side. It looked like a great white shark had taken a bite out of the middle of the big round fish, except, like a cartoon, all the bones were still intact.

"Did a shark bite it?" I asked, naively.

"NO, NO, NO!" yelled Doc. "It's the God-damned sand fleas. Haven't you ever seen a sand flea?" he asked, pointing to a little black dot on the white flesh of the halibut.

"That little thing did *THAT*?" I asked incredulously.

"Yep. There's billions of them down there. The piranhas of the ocean, and if you let your lines soak too long they'll devour your catch."

I actually felt bad for the halibut. Being eaten alive, one little nibble at a time, was no way to die. *Great*, I thought, *now I have those stinkin' sand fleas to worry about too*.

Doc's panic was disconcerting and we watched anxiously as he winched up the next fish.

"Quick, Boy! Grab your gaff!" Doc barked.

Oddly enough, even though it was just six feet away, the next fish, a 120-pound halibut, was in perfect condition. And thus it began. In the next twelve hours, one by one, we proceeded to pull up thousands of pounds of halibut. At one point we were knee deep in halibut ranging in size from fifty to two-hundred-and-fifty pounds.

As I mentioned, this was the first time I'd ever laid eyes on halibut and I was shocked by what an abomination they were. The sight made me question God's infallibility and wonder what cruel joke He was playing when He created this mixed up platypus of the sea. This king of all bottom dwellers grows up to be eight feet long and can weigh five hundred pounds. It looks primordial, with both its dark eyes on one side of its head. The eyes actually migrate after birth, leaving one whole flank completely devoid of color and fins so it can lie flush on the bottom.

And one after another after another they came up in a seemingly endless bounty from the sea. I re-coiled my skates as fast as Doc could winch them up, halting every couple minutes to help him land a big one. As we crossed into the wee hours of the morning, the weather began to worsen with higher wind and harder rain and rougher seas, but onward we marched, foot after foot, yard after yard, mile after mile. The overcast skies made the surroundings visually impenetrable, save the ten feet illuminated by the ship's halogens.

The fish were covering every square inch of deck space and we were forced to stop pulling to let Paul catch up on the cleaning. Doc instructed me to jump down in the fish hold and start packing the cleaned fish with ice. Before leaving port, the hold had been filled with three tons of crushed ice and with all that ice there was not enough room to stand up, so I crawled around from end to end, packing them in, one after another.

"Gentle!" Doc yelled down, "Don't bruise the meat!"

"Okay," I said. I'd never been claustrophobic before, but crawling around those darkened, cramped quarters with all those dead fish staring at me started to creep me out. And I envisioned waves striking the boat and rolling it over, trapping me inside the hull. *Please, Lord,* I thought, *don't let me die down here with these beady-eyed fish.*

In the ever-increasing swell, the *Zimovia* began to roll heavily from side-to-side, causing me great concern and making landing the halibut much more difficult. Doc seemed completely oblivious to the change in weather conditions. There is, I know now, a maniacal giddiness that overcomes a ship's captain in the midst of a fish run. Like a man possessed, Doc stood at the controls in his rain-soaked slickers, with his long-extinguished pipe, just staring wild-eyed into the sea and awaiting its next offering.

With each successive surfacing, he would lean out, swing his gaff, throw a foot up on the bulwark for leverage, and heave the giant fish aboard. With each pull he'd let out a deep, guttural groan. Tempering my own giddiness was the fact that one out of every ten fish had been eaten alive, compounding my fear of being eaten to the bone, one little nibble at a time.

My other duty, which I failed to mention, was to take the recoiled skates, two at a time, from the stern up to the bow. This alone doesn't sound too bad, but each skate weighs thirty to forty pounds, and each trip required me to circumnavigate the wheelhouse where the deck's width was reduced to just fourteen inches and the bulwark came up to slightly below my knees. And to make matters worse, with the ship now rolling side to side in the heavy swell, every journey required me to survive at least one roll towards the cold, dark water. And since both my hands held a skate, there was nothing I could do but arch my back and pray to God. I'm always happy to discover a skill I didn't know I had, so you can imagine my elation upon realizing I could clamp onto smooth steel surfaces using only the cheeks of my ass.

Somewhere around two-thirty in the morning I officially became one of the walking dead despite my long history of all-night partying. Much to Doc's chagrin, I began moving at a snail's pace and routinely gaffing the side of the boat instead of the fish. The skates were no longer recoiling properly and I started tripping and slipping on everything that got in my path. Unfortunately, the fish just kept coming and the rope just kept piling up and the skates just kept needing to be hauled up to the bow. I had never in my life had to work so hard for so long and I started wondering what kind of sadistic bastard came up with the idea of a twenty-four-hour opening. And to think they used to do seventy-two-hour openings.

At that moment, exhausted and covered in blood and guts, I would have traded every dollar I stood to make for a hot shower, clean clothes, and a soft bed. After falling into Doc and accidentally tossing his lucky gaff overboard, he ordered me to go take a nap. I'd like to say I argued with him and refused to go, but as my head hit the pillow and my eyes snapped shut, I remember thinking, *Why in God's name did I ever want to do this?*

After what seemed like a lifetime, I was awakened by the soothing sound of Doc's voice. "Hey, Sleeping Beauty, get your sorry ass up here and help out!"

I came racing up from below feeling somewhat rested and was shocked to discover I'd been sleeping for only an hour and a half. The deck was still covered in fish and the skates were all stacked up, and Doc was still ornery as hell, but at least I was functional again.

Eight miles takes a long time to jog, so you can imagine how long it takes to pull something up from the ocean's bottom ... six feet at a time. Well, I know exactly how long it takes—roughly eleven hours of endless pulling. Daylight arrived and the weather settled down and the sun even peeked out for a while, but still those fish kept coming. Doc started to worry that we wouldn't make the noon deadline, but at eleven o'clock, right on schedule, in calm seas, under a partly cloudy sky, we landed our last fish.

The next several hours were spent cleaning the fish and stowing the gear for the long ride home. We all sang along as Roy Orbison and Charlie Pride (Doc's favorites) blasted over the boat's speakers. The mood on board was nothing short of jubilant. Even Doc chimed in on "Only the Lonely" and "Save the Last Dance for Me."

In hopes of speeding things up, Paul attempted to give me a lesson on fish cleaning, but he wasn't too impressed with my skills. "Son, from the looks of that fish," he said, "you appear to have a bit of a limp wrist."

"Oh, fuck you, Paul," I said. Then old Doc came over and showed off the slow, steady hand of a surgeon.

"See, I'm not just a pretty face," he said, cracking himself up.

## Just for the Halibut

By the time I crawled out of the fish hold for the last time, the sun had set and the temperature had fallen considerably. Paul and I covered the hold and had just finished swabbing the deck when Terry called us in for dinner.

Dinner conversation ranged from halibut to Hemingway, with Doc quoting classics and drawing big laughs with a wild yarn about med school. He had a way of telling a story so that by the end you felt envious, jealous even, wishing you could have been there too—regardless of how badly it ended—and it usually ended badly.

Ignoring Doc's shin kicks, Paul loosed a couple whoppers about the two of them boozing it up while Terry was away at nursing school. She was none too pleased, having assumed he'd been sober the whole time, but what could she do? She just rolled her eyes and he never said a word. Regardless of its pedigree, you don't adopt an old, three-legged dog and then teach it to heel and play dead. It was Doc—and you get what you get.

Even Terry had to admit a few of his of his exploits were pretty funny. Unable to beat them, she joined in with a tale about a drunken Doc attempting a John Wayne impersonation by borrowing Wrangell's only horse, without permission, and marching it up the back steps and into the living room of his house, where he proceeded to accidentally shoot a hole in the floor that ruptured the water pipes. Apparently the guests left shortly thereafter, led by the horse, who took a piece of the doorframe with him.

Figuring that no one could top that one, we called it a night. As the greenhorn, I washed and stowed the dishes,

## The Unnatural Aging of Cheese

then headed below where Paul was already sound asleep. My eyes were shut before my head hit the pillow. The captain just sailed us on home throughout the night.

When we awoke, good old Wrangell was within sight, and I had a mere five hours before my flight was scheduled to leave. But before heading in, we all took a stab at the size of our catch. It was tough to tell, but there had been some real monsters we'd pulled up. One 250-pounder didn't even bite a hook—he'd swallowed, whole, a five-pound red snapper that had swallowed a hook. Terry and Paul thought we'd done pretty well, guessing 14,500 and 15,000 pounds respectively. I didn't have a clue, and Doc, like a good captain, guessed way low, either wanting to avoid disappointment or create more excitement when it sold.

As we pulled up to Wrangell Seafoods, the local fish broker, Doc sent me down in the hold to start handing up fish. Disappointingly, they took a lot less time to offload than they did to catch, so I wondered if Doc hadn't guessed right after all.

After every fish was weighed, a poker-faced man came over and handed Doc a little white slip of paper. A dejected Doc turned to us and said, "Well, I'm sorry to say we did only … SIXTEEN THOUSAND … SIX HUNDRED … AND EIGHTY-FOUR POUNDS! A new personal best!"

As evidenced by the shit-eating grin across the old curmudgeon's face, he thoroughly enjoyed setting us up. *You know*, I thought, *I'm sorta starting to like this crazy pirate.*

We tied up at the Shoemaker Bay marina, where our journey had begun, and started offloading the gear. Two hours later, Terry said—for the sake of the other passengers—that I should probably go get cleaned up. The crew all gathered around me and Doc came out of the wheelhouse with a check in hand. He made a point to remind me that I'd missed the boat prep part of the trip, and now I was gonna miss the clean-up portion, and that I'd gotten to do just the fun stuff.

*Fun stuff,* I thought, *I don't know if I'd call it fun stuff,* but I wasn't about to argue with the man.

"Unfortunately," he said, "those constitute half your deckhand share. That said, however, you didn't do too bad, for an Easterner." He paused, then added, "Thanks to the generosity of your crewmates, and because I'm becoming a softy in my old age, this here is a full deckhand share. We sure hope you had a good time here in Alaska."

Doc handed me a check for $1,750, which is still the most I've ever made for three days' work. It was so unexpected that I didn't really know how to thank them. Paul gave me a bone-crushing fisherman's handshake and said I'd done real good for my first time out.

Trying to pretend his grip wasn't killing me, I said, "Thanks. You take care, Paul."

"You too, Mary Ellen," he replied.

"Fuck you, Paul," I said.

"Fuck you, too, Mary Ellen," he responded.

Part of me could have stayed there and listened to their stories forever. I felt like I'd been granted access to a secret society that most of the world knows nothing about. As they say, the sea is funny thing. It just calls to some men—

men from all walks of life, all sizes and shapes, all races and religions. If you were to monitor the chatter across the Alaska Marine Radio, you'd hear many learned men and women who left great careers to try their hand at harvesting the sea. Most of them would tell you they'd never do anything else again. It's tough, messy, smelly work, but it's rewarding and I understood why they did it. I can't say the sea called to me, but it may have whispered a little.

Terry drove me out to their picturesque three-story log cabin that looked out over Zimovia Straight. After stopping to see the bullet hole and where the horse had once stood, I took the most wonderful shower of my life, using rainwater caught on their roof—a practice not recommended back in New Jersey. Afterwards, I dressed in the best smelling, best feeling clothes I'd ever worn.

"Come on," she said, "We don't want to hit traffic."

"Should I grab tokens for the tolls?" I joked. On the ride over I thanked her profusely for the wonderful experience. Shockingly, we made it in plenty of time for me to catch the lone flight heading south to Seattle. As the Alaska Airlines jet lifted off, I looked down on the little town and somehow I knew I hadn't seen the last of her—and something told me I'd cross paths with old Doc again.

# Jacques Peugeot

**The call came in at O-1500, 18 February 1992.** The young lieutenant said there'd been an uprising in New Orleans and my country needed me.

"I can't," I said, "I've got exams coming up."

"To hell with exams," he exclaimed, "this is far more important."

"Easy for you to say, Mr. West Point Grad," I said.

"Come on," he urged, "we need you down there, soldier."

I said I'd think about it.

"Nothing to think about," he said. "Convoy rolls out at 0600." Then *Bang!* He hung up.

A minute later the phone rang again. "*Cheese,*" he warned, "DON'T—BE—A—COWARD! This may be your only chance to see Mardi Gras. Merriman and my brother already bought tickets. Sludge and Hairball are going … and a bunch of friends from The Point. You don't want to miss this!" he assured me. And *Bang!* He hung up again.

Ten seconds later the phone rang a third time. "Cheese," he said, "you know they show their tits, right?"

## The Unnatural Aging of Cheese

"Yeah," I said, "I know."

"*For just beads*, Cheese," he said.

"Yeah, I know," I said.

"Well, me and the boys got a trunk full of beads!" he said. "There won't be a covered set in the city. *Guaranteed!*"

"All right, okay already, I'll try calling my dad."

With a three-year-late start on college, I had finally met a nice girl, settled down, and hit the books—also shedding my party-boy reputation in the process. And I wasn't about to risk it all for a chance to go drinking, regardless of how rare an opportunity it might be.

I reminded myself to keep focused on the future and to be responsible. Suddenly, like phantom sensations in the missing limbs of an amputee, I felt that old irrepressible urge to party. It welled up inside me. Doing as the counselor had instructed, I took several deep breaths, shut my eyes, and visualized all the wonderful things I enjoyed about the new healthier life I was leading. Since I'd started employing the powers of meditation and visualization, my life had changed dramatically.

"Are you going to class?" my girlfriend asked.

"No, I'm going to Mardi Gras," I told her, "see you in six days."

For obvious reasons, I didn't wait around for her reaction.

Having a father who was an airline pilot could come in pretty handy, but since we flew standby, we were always subject to seating availability. My father had said my only chance of getting to New Orleans was a 7:15 p.m. flight out of PDX. He asked me how far I was from Portland.

## Jacques Peugeot

"About four and a half hours," I said.

"You'll never make it," he said, "that flight takes off in five and a half hours."

"Oh, I'll make it," I said, "trust me."

"Hey," he said, "don't you have exams coming up?"

Caught off guard by his impromptu probe, I quickly ran through every possible response and eventually settled on—"Nope."

Twenty minutes later, with hastily stuffed bag in hand, I stood at the door to Jacques Peugeot, my sleek French-made 505 Turbo Peugeot. I paused a moment to assess his condition. *What a piece of shit*, I thought to myself. Jacques had been a gift from my father, who, under the heavy influence of alcohol, had bet me a car that I'd never get straight A's. But after an art and music appreciation class, to his dismay he found himself wandering the grounds of a used car lot with me. Of course I passed by all the practical vehicles with their spotless maintenance logs and high mpg, and went straight for the most unique car on the lot, the Turbo Peugeot, which would later come to be known as "Jacques."

From the day we arrived home, Jacques suffered an endless string of ailments, which gobbled up more of my beer money than I care to discuss. And judging by the inaccessibility of parts, there's little doubt that I owned the only French-made automobile between Portland and San Francisco. I knew the odds of making Mardi Gras were not good, but it was like all that beer and all those bare breasts were crying out to me from across the country. And to a professional partier like me, going to Mardi Gras was like a holy trek to Mecca. You had to go once in your lifetime, or at least die trying. *What sort of man would I be*, I wondered, *if I didn't at least try?* On my third attempt he turned over, kicked out a large ball of white smoke, and achieved a somewhat sickly idle.

I'd like to say we raced down the onramp, but Jacques' turbo had failed just three weeks after bringing him home, rendering him a 4-cylinder with the rapid acceleration of a glacier. However, with the help of gravity and a strong tail wind, we did manage to make our way up to 65 mph. Heading north out of Ashland, Oregon, we crossed the long flat Rogue Valley before entering the southernmost mountains of the Western Cascades.

Somewhere around Wolf Creek, as Jacques struggled up a steep slope, a light rain began to fall. A short time later it converted to a rain-snow mix, which was a bit concerning because Jacques had the balance and traction of a newborn fawn on a frozen pond.

Regardless, I was making good time and I had just drifted into a fantasy about a Cajun coed, who was only moments from exposing a dandy set of double-D's, when all of a sudden the driver-side windshield wiper came sweeping up and flopped off the outer edge of my windshield. And there it stayed, stuck, with its little motor just whirring away. *What the hell?* I thought to myself. Snowflakes began accumulating quickly, blurring my vision and making driving nearly impossible. Acting on impulse, I manually rolled down the window, stuck my hand out into the freezing wind, and shoved the wiper back on, where—thankfully—it resumed its wiping. Disaster averted, I withdrew my cold, wet hand and rolled up the window.

All was well for about five wipes, but on the sixth, the wiper came up and flopped off the side again. "Cam own, Jacques, ziss eez noot foonay!" I said, rolling down the window a second time. And again I reached out and popped it back on, where again it resumed its wiping ... just long enough for me to get the window back up and then off the side it went. And so it went, for the next thirty minutes, up and down went the window, in and out went my hand, until my hand had turned a most unnatural shade of red. Having just completed a course in statistical probability, I wondered what the odds were of something like this occurring. Having gotten a "D," I was completely incapable of actually calculating those odds, but suffice it to say that I presumed them to be *quite* long. "Cam own, Jacques," I cried, "why-ah yoo dwing ziss tow may?"

Unfortunately, Jacques responded by causing the wiper to flop off every fourth wipe, which hardly left me enough time to roll the window back up before having to roll it back down again. Knowing how temperamental the French can be, I decided to try a new, gentler approach.

"Jacques! Yoo, pessa sheet, yoo! Ziss eez noot foonay!" I cried, slamming my fist down on the dash. At that point, the wiper started flopping off on every single wipe, which essentially left me no choice but to permanently leave my hand out the window. I rolled it down just enough to fit my hand, wrist, and a portion of my forearm out, but still the noise and frigid wind were unbearable, and I could see my

## The Unnatural Aging of Cheese

own breath every time I cursed Jacques' name. In an attempt to stave off hypothermia, I cranked up the heater, having forgotten it quit working sometime after the air conditioning, just prior to the turbo's last push. With each impact, I felt sure my hand would shatter, and with three and a half hours left in my journey, something needed to be done or I might never again hold a drink in my left hand.

You don't typically bring winter gloves with you to Southern Louisiana, so while holding my left hand out the window and steering with my knee, I reached in the back for the *next best thing*. Five minutes later, with my arm safely encased in three pairs of elbow-high tube socks, I stuck my hand back out the window.

"Aha, Jacques!" I said, "Ziss rown goose tow may! Ha! Ha!"

It was too dark to see their faces, but some of the passing drivers had to be wondering why I was driving in a freezing rainstorm—in February—with my broken arm sticking out the window. However, they probably just assumed that was standard behavior for anyone dumb enough to buy a French car.

Life was less miserable for the next twenty minutes, but, eventually, even my six layers of socks proved no match for Mother Nature, and I found myself groping around the back for more protection. I'd only brought the three pairs of socks and I was in no position to be particular, so, grabbing the first thing I found, I cinched the elastic waistband around my wrist and thrust it back out the window. In hindsight, I should've anticipated the potential parachute effect caused by a 65 mph wind, but sadly, I did not. If you're like me and you've spent countless hours wondering how an orphaned pink flip-flop or a single red mitten ends up on the shoulder of some lonely stretch of highway, well, you're now privy to the peculiar turn of events that deposited one pair of large white underpants into the passing lane of Interstate-5 somewhere outside of Drain, Oregon.

Disappointed by my loss but undeterred, I reached back again. And although I didn't litter the highway with anymore clothing, by the time I'd reached Cottage Grove, every article of clothing I'd brought was lying in a wet heap behind the passenger seat. Unfortunately, while I struggled to figure out how to make one pair of underpants last six days in humid weather, Jacques' wiper went sweeping down the windshield and decided not to make the return trip.

"Jaaaaaaacques! Zase ez SABO--TAGE!" I cried, shaking my fist in the air. "Pleez, Jacques, I beeg of yoo, doe noot doe zase tow may."

I waited a few seconds, hoping he might reconsider, but that wiper didn't budge, and with no possible way of reaching it, I was forced to pull over. As we came to a halt, I envisioned my flight fading into the horizon and taking with it any chance of me seeing all those naked breasts.

"Yoo boss-taird, Jacques," I said, "I wee getch-yoo faw zees!"

Realizing my window was waning, I jumped out of Jacques, leaned over the windshield, and quickly determined that I knew nothing about how windshield wipers worked—and even less about how to repair them. However—hearing the little motor running—I reached down and gave the wiper a nudge. As I did, it started back up the window normally but then flopped off the outer edge. With my right hand I lifted it back on the glass and it immediately headed south, where it was blocked by my left hand and headed back up again. As long as I kept my hands on either end of its arc, why, it worked perfectly. *Now*, I thought, *if I only had someone to drive while I lie on the hood and keep this wiper working.* Since that wasn't really an option, I reached in and turned off the engine.

As I paced back and forth on the shoulder of I-5, I racked my brain for a solution, but after ten minutes, I had nothing and I realized my trip was probably over. Dejected, I started back towards the car to flip on my hazard lights and hope somebody would stop and give me a ride to a phone booth. At that moment, I would have given anything to curse him in his own native tongue, but, as luck would have it, I'd taken four years of Spanish. As if enough hadn't gone wrong already, on my way back to the car, I tripped over my own shoelace and nearly took a header into the drainage ditch. *What a night this has been!* I thought, *Lord, help me.*

And that is *precisely* what He did.

Having been raised in Philadelphia and New Jersey, the only logical explanation is that I channeled the inventive spirits of Ben Franklin or Thomas Edison. Stripping the lace from my shoe, I quickly tied one end around the wiper blade and strung the other end through the gap in the driver's side window. Energized by a newfound sense of hope, I climbed back behind the wheel. With one hand encased in wet socks and the other needed for driving, I had no choice but to use the only body part left available. As you might imagine, the flavor of a year old shoelace leaves something to be desired, but desperate times call for desperate measures, so I laid it across my lower jaw and clamped down tight. Obviously my plan was to use my sock arm to block the outer flop, and then when the wiper stuck at the bottom, I intended to snap my head to the right, which in theory was going to yank the lace hard enough to get the wiper moving up again.

As foolproof as the plan seemed, I thought a stationary test run might be in order. Scooting my seat all the way forward, I stuck my sock arm back out the window, turned on the ignition, and with hopeful anticipation, flipped on the wipers. Watching anxiously as it completed its upward arc, I knew any chance of me making that flight rested on the frayed threads of that dirty old lace.

"Plez, Jacques," I muttered through gritted teeth, "danoot fay me naw, ma frawn."

Hitting my sock hand, the wiper reversed course and headed down. *This is it*, I thought. *This is the moment of truth*. Luckily the shoelace proved plenty strong. However, my brain did not have enough time to notify my jaw that the lace was not long enough. So, when it got about halfway down, it pulled taught, first slamming my forehead into the roof support and then attempting to pull my whole head through that little gap in the window. You'd be amazed how powerful a wiper motors is, and for a moment, we were engaged in life and death tug-o-war. And then—just before the window or my skull was about to shatter—that lace was violently ripped from my still-clenched jaw.

It took a moment to regain my senses and check for missing teeth. As I rubbed the new knot on my forehead, I said, "Oh, zat hut, Jacques. Zat was noot ah nize sing too doo. Zat's eet, Jacques! Yoo or noot ma frawn enny-MO!"

As they say, necessity is the mother invention, so after regaining my composure, I stripped the lace from my other shoe and tied the two together. In my next test I had too much slack, but after a couple tries, I got the hang of it. Unfortunately, due to the distance it had to travel, I was forced to supply so much slack that my head was practically lying in the passenger seat to provide enough torque. To be perfectly honest, it wasn't the easiest motion to perform, and that was sitting still, so I had some doubts as to whether I'd be able to keep it up for two and a half hours driving 65 mph down a dark, wet highway—but I had to try.

"Uh-kay, Jacques," I said, "less tick et sloo."

Waiting for a break in the cars, I carefully pulled into the slow lane. It was extremely difficult to stay in my lane when performing the jerking motion, but gradually I started to get control and worked my way back up to 65 mph.

"Ahhhh, merci beaucoup, Jacques" I said.

I'm not sure if it was the excitement of being back in the race, or if I just yanked too hard, but the next thing I knew, the blade detached from its base and started rolling up my windshield. My heart jumped in my throat and time slowed down. *No, no, no, no,* I thought, *this can't be happening.* Panic set in and with each passing second, I saw my Mardi Gras trip rolling away.

Survival mode kicked in, and, acting on instinct, I shot forward, practically pressing my face to the inside of the windshield. Extending my sock arm as far out of the car as possible, I somehow managed to pin the wiper to the glass—by its very tip. *Oh, thank God*, I thought. But with my hand encased in socks, I had no ability to actually grab it. During the commotion I had been weaving all over the road, so I attempted to regain control.

And that's when it slipped. In abject terror, I watched my hope roll up the rest of the window and onto Jacques' roof. *Well, that does it*, I thought.

Suddenly I felt a little tug on my jaw, and then, in the corner of my eye, saw something drop down the side of the car. And then I could feel the tension in my jaw as the lace went taught. In my panic, I had forgotten the shoelace in my mouth, which was still attached to the blade like a lifeline. But now it hung precariously, like a fish on string, just inches above the road. *Oh, my God! Oh, my God!* I thought, *I still got it!* Shifting into neutral, I rolled the wheel to the right and made a b-line for the shoulder of the highway.

Jumping out, I untied the blade, gave it a cursory examination, and was thrilled to discover that reattaching a wiper blade is an action even an idiot like me could perform. Acutely aware that these repeated pit stops were costing me valuable time, I quickly retied the lace further down towards the base this time, strung it back through the window and leaped inside the car.

## The Unnatural Aging of Cheese

Before pulling back onto the highway, I said, "Less gee sum-sing stray hair, Jacques. I wheel-be gow-eeng to zee Mardi Gras, oh yoo wheel-be dry-veeng wiss ziss why-pair sue faw oop yaw eggs-hoost Pie-ipp, yoo wheel feel zee pray-sure awn yaw front boomp-pair!"

And with that, I pulled out onto the highway.

The next two hours went smoothly—well, as smoothly as possible when having to jerk my head to the right every three seconds. It takes extreme concentration to drive a vehicle like that, but once I got rolling there was no stopping me. I could almost smell that Jambalaya cooking.

As you might imagine, once I entered well-lit city limits, I started getting some strange looks. One can only imagine what other drivers were thinking—perhaps I was a nearsighted, epileptic with a broken arm who had just farted. But that's just a guess. When a carload of teenagers drove by laughing and honking their horn, I thought about flipping them the bird but decided to take the high road, in part because it was the right thing to do and in part because my free hand was encased in six pairs of socks.

It is a reach to describe a 4-cylinder, turbo-less Peugeot as lightning fast, but that is what it was. I don't know if France has ever conducted any 4-cylinder Peugeot races, but I'm pretty sure I'd dominate if they did ... at least in the one-armed, wiperless division.

Fifteen minutes before my flight was scheduled to take off, I skidded into a parking space in the expensive short-term parking structure. With no clothing left to speak of, and no time to reclaim my shoelaces, I snatched my shaving

## Jacques Peugeot

kit and toothbrush out of the back and took off for the gate—stopping just long enough to kick Jacques in the door panel and stub my toe.

As I hobbled off I yelled, "Au revoir, Jacques, yoo pessa sheet. Ah ween!"

# The Short Arm of the Law

The fugitive could be heard scurrying towards the darkened laundry room where he had been known to hide from the short arm of the law. A less seasoned tracker would have lost his trail, but not this relentless little peacekeeper. She'd been hunting outlaws since she was in diapers, and knowing the importance of traveling light, she headed off wearing only a little pair of pastel undypants and a pink cowboy hat. Having followed his trail to the edge of the darkness, the three-year-old Little Deputy now entered armed with a plastic white hanger in one hand and a half-eaten cracker in the other.

Had he fallen for the winding trail of dog biscuits leading to the overturned playpen, she would not have been in this dangerous predicament. However, this wasn't their first run-in together, and Little Deputy was known to giggle in the face of danger. So with ice-cold milk in her veins, she cornered the bandit and closed in.

"Come wiff me, Buds. Yaw goin' to jay-wool," she said.

At the sound of her voice, a high-pitched whine was

emitted from somewhere between the washer and dryer. Like a trapped rat, his eyes darted around the room frantically searching for a way out. But in his heart, he knew she always got her dog. He whimpered shamelessly for his freedom, but the law was the law, and Little Deputy took him into custody. Hooking her plastic hanger through his red collar, she began dragging him away.

Determined not to make it easy, the aforementioned Buds, who will henceforth be referred to by his outlaw name of diabolical "Black Buds," sat back on his haunches, stiffened his legs, and ground his sharp nails into the floor. An unpleasant scratching could be heard as Little Deputy forcibly dragged him across the stick-resistant linoleum of the laundry room and into the hardwood forest of the kitchen. Outweighing her by nearly twenty pounds, Black Buds' four legs and muscular physique were still no match for Little Deputy's fleshy flat feet, opposable thumbs, and three-year-old determination. Bending, but not breaking, the flimsy white hanger shook under the incredible tension, stretching to what seemed an impossible length. Black Buds prayed for a nice shag carpet to latch into, but Little Deputy continued her march towards jail, halting momentarily only when the dog managed to take cover behind the wastebasket and under a kitchen chair.

At one point, a couple of townsfolk who bore a striking resemblance to the Little Deputy's mom and dad called out, "Hey, Honey, what did he do?"

Her birth name was Cheney Lane Chrisman, but the townsfolk all knew her as Honey. Unwilling to share any details, and possibly fearful of compromising Black Buds' chance for a fair trial, the young deputy would only say, "I'm takin' Buddy to jay-wool."

"Yeah, but what did Buddy do, Honey?" the townsfolk persisted.

Unwilling to release a single fact in the case, she would say, "Buddy's bay-add and he's goin' to jay-wool."

And at that the eternal tug-o-war between good and evil played out on the kitchen floor, with Black Buds looking pleadingly at the townsfolk, praying that they might intervene, but alas, he soon realized his fate was sealed.

In all fairness to Black Buds, he gave a valiant effort through most of the kitchen, but once the struggle crossed onto the expansive pinewood plains of the living room, the outcome seemed almost a foregone conclusion. However, as he slid through the narrow canyon between the couch and the chaise lounge, also known as "Throw Pillow Pass," Black Buds seized upon his final chance for escape. Having bided his time, he launched one final counter-offensive.

Calling on the forces of gravity and friction, Black Buds leaned back at a 45-degree angle, locked his four knees tightly, clenched his teeth, and ground his furry buttocks into the floor until their progress came to a screeching halt.

Little Deputy was clearly frustrated by this latest attempt at escape, but glaring back with a "resistance is futile" look, she called on what seemed an innate understanding of the laws of physics. Leaning in the opposite direction, with her face just inches from the ground, she began grunting and heaving and pumping her legs. And although she was greatly outweighed, and the hanger seemed on the verge of snapping, the balance of power slowly shifted in her favor. Almost imperceptibly at first, they began to move again. With his will broken and all hope lost, Black Buds stood up begrudgingly, leaving an outline of dust bunnies in his place, and walked willingly through the jailhouse door.

Once inside the bedroom, Little Deputy carefully hung the hanger over a dresser knob, then turned tail and sprinted out, slamming the accordion door shut, and plopping down in front of it before the fugitive set himself free. Stopping to wipe her little brow, she took a moment to savor the victory.

From inside the cell came a series of piteous whines and then ... nothing. Absolute silence. Not a sound could be heard, which seemed to confuse Little Deputy. She fought the urge for a moment, but then curiosity got the best of her, so she hopped up to check on the prisoner. Unable to see much through the slats in the door, she cracked it open about two inches and pressed an eye to the gap. This was just the opportunity the prisoner had been waiting for.

Little Deputy was hit one, two, three times in the face with a lighting fast five-inch tongue. Reeling backward, she fell to the floor, hat knocked clean off her head, and there she sat, frantically wiping slobber from her face. His charcoal black nose already through the gap, Black Buds very adeptly slid open the door, leapt over the disoriented deputy, skittered across the living room, skidded into the kitchen door, scraped his way across the laundry room linoleum, and raced out the back door, which had been left open by

## The Unnatural Aging of Cheese

the kindly townsfolk who'd failed to help him previously.

Meanwhile, back in the living room, Little Deputy regained her composure. Jumping to her feet, she replaced her hat, hiked up her undies, and shortly thereafter the sound of tender little feet could be heard pitter patting at high speed through the living room, across the kitchen, and into the laundry room, where she cast an accusatory glare at the simple townsfolk standing nearby.

Leaning out the back door, she yelled, "Noooo, Budsy, comb baaaack! You ... have ... to ... go ... to ... jay-wool, Budsy!"

But sadly enough ... it was too late. Having tasted the sweet air of freedom, Black Buds was gone, escaped into the wilds of the back yard, and never to be seen again. Or at least not until suppertime.

That evening, a delicate tiny hand appeared under the table with a quarter of a grilled cheese sandwich and then a green bean, and Black Buds pulled back his lips, exposing his sharp white teeth. He ever so gently removed the tasty treat from the fingers, taking special care not to bite the hand that fed him.

Ol' Buddy is salt and peppered now, and a little arthritic. He hides during the day but always returns at night to sleep by the bed of Little Deputy. Over the years he's suffered all manner of indignities: dresses, pants, bottle-feedings, bonnet-wearings, even a mismatched sock or two. He has been known to carry as many as four Barbie dolls riding bareback at one time, sometimes wearing a dishtowel cape tucked in his collar for flying.

### The Short Arm of the Law

As friends, Little Deputy and Buddy have traveled to far off lands and distant worlds, even to the bottom of the sea. Only stopping for a snack, they've fought off ghosts and pirates and aliens, and saved the world ... repeatedly. Despite all the indignities, Buddy gets handsomely rewarded, receiving roughly half of every meal she has eaten. Little Deputy may not remember all their adventures when she's grown, but the love they shared has left an indelible mark. Buddy will be gone someday soon, but in a real sense, he is eternal.

# Funeral Traditions

"**B**urn 'um and urn 'um! Char 'um and jar 'um!"
That's the refrain my family chants when you die.
Whatever Old World German customs we brought over in 1739 were long ago replaced by more practical concerns, like expediency and expense.

Grandpa's dying wish was to have his airline pilot son sprinkle him over the Pacific Ocean. However, knowing my tight-fisted father, he'd be lucky if he got flushed down a lavatory somewhere over Sioux City, Iowa. That said, you can imagine my awkwardness when my wife's family invited me out to the old Indian graveyard to take part in her grandfather's traditional burial. Furthering my angst was the fact that not two weeks prior, my aunt had discovered that we are distant relatives of one General George Armstrong Custer, a little known fact I wish she had kept to herself.

Risking the appearance of insensitivity, I openly confessed my deep-seeded reservations, but my wife assured me it was an honor just to be asked, and that nobody would know about that Custer connection, and, most importantly,

## Funeral Traditions

it would really mean a lot to her if I participated. So the next day, with shovel in hand, I headed off for the old Indian cemetery, not really knowing what to expect.

Once there, I was told to report to her Great Uncle Phil, the family patriarch. Uncle Phil was a short, stocky, ex-military man, who had to be on the far side of seventy-five, but looked like he could whip everyone else with one hand tied behind his back.

As I approached, I found every male under the age of forty assembled around a rectangular wooden frame lying on the ground. Every male, that is, except Ketchikan Sam, my wife's crazy cousin from Alaska. The Tribe had nicknamed Sam the "Indian Elvis" because he reportedly bore a striking resemblance to young Mr. Presley himself, except he was shorter and, of course, a little darker skinned. Anyways, Elvis had apparently left the building but he had not headed to the cemetery, so a red-faced Great Uncle Phil stormed off after him.

Well, they must have just missed each other because right after Uncle Phil left, a four-wheel drive pickup came rip roarin' up the hill and to my great surprise, behind the wheel sat what appeared to be a pint-sized Indian Elvis. And just like the real Elvis would have done, he showed up with the truck bed full of cheap canned beer. Now, just so you know, most of the Tribal Elders abhor alcohol and they had expressly forbidden it from entering the graveyard. That said, none of those fellas there were Elders, and I think they figured since Elvis went to all the trouble of smuggling it up, why, there was no good sensible reason to let it all go to waste. And as for me, well, being of German descent, they didn't have to ask me twice to wet my palate.

I must admit that when I first arrived at the cemetery, I was a little nervous because, as hard as I tried not to notice, me and my brother-in-law, Mikey, were the only two white folks in attendance. But, beer being the great unifying force that it is, it wasn't long before I couldn't tell whether we were on an Indian reservation in Oregon or right back in my native New Jersey, where the only thing Indian is the name of the towns. Those Indians weren't so different after all. They all liked cold beer, just like back in Jersey. And they all liked insulting each other, just like back in Jersey. And just like back in Jersey, they all went by nicknames.

There was the aforementioned Elvis, and cousin Two Flush (don't ask), Jim-Jim, Sammy the Rake, Potato Bill Sanchez, Little Philly and Big Philly, just to name a few. And by our third beer together, why, we were like brothers, and they had even given me and Mikey our very own Indian names. Mikey didn't care much for Butternut, but I felt my name, Snowflake, had a quiet kind of dignity.

Well, just about that time, Great Uncle Phil returned and, let me tell you—he *was* an Elder, and he was none too happy about the party that had broken out at his brother's future gravesite. After calling Elvis a good-for-nothing dumb son-of-a-bitch, he made an attempt to round up all the beer, but quickly realized that particular cat wasn't going back into the bag.

So then he ordered us—"us" being a "bunch of useless bull tits" as he put it—to grab our shovels and line up in

## Funeral Traditions

pairs. He then stepped forward, made a short prayer in some ancient Indian tongue, and dug the first ceremonial shovel of dirt. I hadn't noticed it before, but as me and Butternut got in line, we were nearly a foot taller than everyone else. Except for cousin Two Flush, who was a six-footer, Great Uncle Phil was the giant of the group at five-feet-five.

Suddenly, I recalled my wife telling me that a couple generations back, her relatives had intermarried with some Filipinos, leaving a tribe of near Lilliputians. Clearly Mikey and I stuck out like a couple of jolly white giants standing there in line, and when Great Uncle Phil asked if we'd been held back a couple grades, why, it fetched a pretty hearty chuckle from the group. However, men are more than their physical stature, so we tried hard not to stare and just awaited our turn to dig.

Now, let me tell you that digging graves is hard work, so don't ever let Hollywood fool you with their cut-to-the-finish editing. It wasn't long before every one of us was a sweaty, dirty mess, but we were making good progress ... at first, anyway. However, by the time we got down about four feet it became evident that my vertically challenged compatriots were beginning to experience a severe mechanical disadvantage. Some of them had to reach so high to get the dirt out of the hole that it slowed down our progress. Finally, Great Uncle Phil had seen enough, so at the four-and-a-half-foot mark, he began kicking guys out of the rotation in an ascending order from shortest to tallest.

First went Little Philly, Sammy the Rake, and Bartholomew Big Bear, who was much wider than he was tall. At the

## The Unnatural Aging of Cheese

five-foot mark, we lost Martin Black Crow, Wendell Whitefeather, and Big Philly, who really couldn't have been more than an inch taller than Little Philly. And so it went, every couple of inches, until it got down to just two teams: Me and Butternut, and Great Uncle Phil and cousin Two Flush. Needless to say, our reduced numbers put a real strain on the rotation, but we continued along undaunted. And we were making good progress … until Uncle Phil's sciatic nerve acted up, which caused him to hit Two Flush in the foot with his shovel, which in turn left just me and Butternut to finish those last six inches alone.

Six feet is a long way down, and the earth's layers change a lot in that distance, as do the people digging it. It's been my experience that Indians are generally a festive bunch, and the thirty or so Indians surrounding the grave I was standing in seemed to be having a pretty good time, maybe a little too good of a time. That said, digging graves is monotonous work, and a man's mind tends to wander, especially when he's drinking beer and doing strenuous exercise under the hot August sun.

Unfortunately, mine wandered right back to my aunt telling me about our General Custer connection, and that's when their laughing and carrying on began to take on a more ominous tone. I tried to wash the thought from my mind and dismiss it as coincidence, but the irony of two white guys standing at the bottom of a grave they'd just dug, surrounded by a bunch of cackling Indians, was somewhat hard to ignore. I don't know who made the first Custer's Last Stand joke, but needless to say, I was not laughing.

## Funeral Traditions

Now, my father didn't raise no fool, so I fully realized that I'd been hoodwinked. Here I thought I was doing a good deed by helping to dig this old Indian man's grave and doing my part to heal the wounds of history, only to find out it had all been a rouse to trick me into digging my own grave. I don't know which stung more, the realization that I'd been tricked, or that my double-crossing wife had suffered through six long years of marriage just to get me in that position. That said, my family is a lot of things, but we're not quitters, and although horribly outnumbered there was no way I was going out without a fight. After all, there were two of us, and with three cans of warm beer, two shovels, and a set of car keys, it wasn't like we were unarmed.

Suffice it to say, no one will ever cut a finger on Butternut's sharp intellect, and try as I might to warn him, I just couldn't get him to understand my ventriloquistic whispers. He kept asking, "What onions are going to kill us?"

I became concerned he might tip off the onions, so I came to the difficult conclusion that it was every white man for himself. As we finished squaring up the sides of that grave, I formulated my plan for a solo escape.

I am not proud of what happened next, but if my dim-witted brother-in-law had not bent over to dig out a rock, I would not have felt compelled to step onto his back, and if he had not reared up in surprise, I would not have been compelled to plant a second foot on the top of his head and thrust myself up and out of that grave, where I belly-flopped onto the sweet-smelling grass of freedom. The stunned Indians quickly closed in around me, blotting out the sun, and I could feel their hands grasping and clawing at me. But through a sea of short little legs and stubby feet I could see the light of salvation shining and I refused to be taken alive. Getting on all fours, I began to crawl at a blistering pace. I don't know how I survived that gauntlet of angry Fili-Pindians, but after what seemed an eternity, I crawled through a little pair of stonewashed Levi's and burst forth into the life-giving light of day.

Wasting no time at all, I leapt to my feet and sprinted towards the distant tree line. I was too afraid to look back, but I heard their hoots and hollers, their taunts of "Run, Snowflake, Run," and the whistles of what must have been poison-tipped arrows shot in my direction. I honestly don't know how many followed me, but somehow I managed to lose them all. The following twelve hours are a bit of a blur, but I arrived home early the next morning, suffering from mild exposure, all manner of scrapes and bruises, and a world-class case of poison oak. Needless-to-say, my wife was shocked at my appearance and asked where in God's name I had been. However, I saw right through her thin veil of deceit, and despite my utter exhaustion, I wasted no time in confronting her about her treachery, an accusation she flatly denied.

Two Flush and Great Uncle Phil dropped my car off the next day. My wife told them I was sleeping. But I listened quietly as Uncle Phil explained my peculiar behavior the day prior—how I'd climbed up poor Butternut's back, how I'd crawled away like a madman, how they tried to help me up, how I'd run off into the forest in a bizarre zigzagging

## Funeral Traditions

pattern. He said they'd all whistled for me to come back, but I just kept right on running. Great Uncle Phil said he appreciated all my hard work, but he strongly recommended she keep me off the firewater in the future. He even gave her the card of his psychotherapist niece in suburban Portland, and then hugged her goodbye. My wife gave me a disgusted look as she entered the bedroom, but in my mind, each race deals with death in its own way.

I guess we Germans tend to run from it.

Peeking through the blinds, I saw Great Uncle Phil walking away, shaking his head. I heard him say, "You know, Two Flush, juss when you tink you got dem white people figgered out...."

# Toss the Meat

**Meat might be what's for dinner** at other homes, but you'd serve yourself well to stay clear of it at mine. My wife is a kind and sweet woman, but we must have eaten out a lot before marriage, because I would remember cooking this bad if I'd tasted it.

The only thing worse than eating one of her meals is the memory of having eaten more than one. Dinner gets ruined with such regularity that she's either incredibly passive aggressive, or I horribly wronged her in a past life, and this is some sort of karmic retribution.

The children and I affectionately refer to her kitchen as "The Crematorium." Cajuns would undoubtedly grow tired of that much blackening. Why we have an oven timer is a mystery to me, as she seems far more comfortable letting smoke alarms serve in that capacity. Between the constant alarms and the drone of the hood fan, one can hardly hear himself think. The din was once unbearable, but it's now dinner music in our home.

Off the top of my head, I cannot recall a meal she has

## Toss the Meat

not botched. Certainly chicken and beef have taken the brunt of her abuse, but in all fairness, fish has suffered greatly as well. And then there's pork. Poor, poor, pork! She has committed unspeakable atrocities against pork. She tends to err on the side of overcooking, and like the poor unsuspecting citizens of Pompeii, she often superheats food, evaporating all moisture in just a nanosecond, and leaving the poor creature a rock-hard lump of charcoal-black ash, essentially mummified, its little spirit trapped between this world and the next.

As you might imagine, what to do with all these indigestible entrees became a real problem. I tried to dispose of them in the usual way, but having grown tired of giving our dogs the Heimlich maneuver, I quietly began tossing the burnt offerings off the back porch in hopes the creatures of the forest might scavenge them. However, this did not prove to be the case. Oh sure, a few of the creatures built crude shelters, and the raccoon living under our house wheeled a pizza in front her hole for protection; but overall, the meat mummies were accumulating faster than we could dispose of them. When a large raven dented the hood of my car trying to fly off with our Thanksgiving turkey, it became clear that something needed to be done.

Quite by accident, the kids and I discovered that most of the entrees, or ash-trees as we like to call them, would disintegrate when they hit the back fence with enough velocity. Using what was once a perfectly edible chicken wing, we etched a crude bulls eye and began a nightly ritual of "Huck the Ham," "Toss the T-Bone," "Chuck the Chicken," "Pitch

## The Unnatural Aging of Cheese

the Pork"... you get the idea. Well, as you might imagine, it was surprisingly difficult to hit the target, primarily due to the irregular shape of most cuts of meat. Take your average store-bought strip steak, for instance. The trick is to sidearm it at a pretty severe angle to prevent it from hooking away like a boomerang and missing the target entirely. Anyone who's had occasion to throw a strip steak knows what I'm talking about.

Some entrees would hit with a thunk and bounce back but, to our great delight, most would explode into little clouds of black dust, leaving a fortuitous smudge on the fence, which greatly helped mediate any scoring disputes.

As you may have guessed, some meats proved more suitable for tossing than others. For example, my wife made a leg of lamb last Easter that knocked two planks off the fence and tumbled into the neighbor's yard. Certainly no harm had been intended, but the neighbor promptly attached a nasty note and heaved it back over, shattering my ceramic birdbath. My oldest daughter was pretty shaken up by the whole exchange, but I assured her that he was probably still upset about the errant pork chop that took out his picture window last winter. The fact of the matter is that pork chops tend to float on you, and if he'd ever taken the time to throw one, he would be much more sympathetic.

Anyways, in case you are competitive like us, Cornish hens tend to be the best, because they're somewhat spherical, and by the time my wife's done with them, they are roughly the size of a baseball. Some folks might not be appreciative of our brand of fun, but my parents raised me to

## Toss the Meat

make the best of any situation. After all, the game is both challenging and educational. It taught the children all about aerodynamics: lift and drag, accounting for crosswinds, not to mention arithmetic. Understandably, food tossing is not for everyone, however the kids and I sure enjoy it, and most importantly, it takes our minds off the hunger.

# The Pampered Pooch

**Not long ago, our dog,** or I should say my *wife's* dog, conveniently developed a handful of very debilitating physical and psychological illnesses. Severe claustrophobia struck first, and he was no longer able to stay in the suffocating confines of the carpeted doghouse I'd built for him in the backyard. At first we thought he was afraid of the dark, but after running electricity out there to install a night-light, he still refused to enter.

Next, we bought him one of those really plush dog beds, some might call it a throne, and set up a nice space for him in the garage but alas, this, too, proved an unacceptable and overly snug environment for our, I mean *her*, persnickety pooch. All night long, he would scratch at the garage door and cry and whine until some softhearted individual, usually my wife or my seven-year-old daughter, would go and let him in. Against my wishes, I might add.

You see, unlike them, I saw through his poorly thought out ploy. As the dog's name, Thurston P. Snuffington III, implies, my wife has always pampered the mangy mutt, but

## The Pampered Pooch

this latest coddling was just unacceptable. Clearly, the dog was slowly but surely attempting to make his way into the house. Meanwhile, our other dog, *my* dog, was stuck out in the backyard, sleeping in a *doghouse* of all things, and not complaining about it, either.

*Her* dog just happens to have a severe case of late-onset claustrophobia, which no one seemed to find the least bit suspicious. No one except me, that is. I was on to his little charade, for all the good it did me.

Anyway, once he breached the outer skin of the home, we … I … tried penning him in the kitchen using our two-year-old's baby gates. Not surprisingly, he whined and cried all night until some big, unnamed softy released him from his tiled jail cell. She said the tile was too cold for the dog's feet and that he was bothered by the smell of all the cleaning products. I told her there were none of those things in the backyard, but, needless to say, he soon took up residence in the living room where, admittedly, he seemed happy. For a while. However, never satisfied, the dog began shunning his name-brand doggy bed and instead made himself nice and comfortable on our new couch, pulling off all my carefully placed obstructions.

Meanwhile, *my* poor dog was sleeping soundly in the dreadfully inhospitable backyard and not making so much as a peep about the blatant inequality being exhibited.

Well, about the time we started thinking my wife's dog was settled and the rest of the family could finally get a good night's rest, he started exhibiting a whole new set of bothersome behaviors.

## The Unnatural Aging of Cheese

First off, he suffered horrible separation anxiety whenever we left the house, or, more accurately, whenever my wife left. He would tip over the trash and tear up the house. The neighbors said they could hear him in there all day, just crying and wailing until my wife's eventual return.

Then came a dreadful case of agoraphobia, which prevented him from going outside at all. Ever. He just flatly refused. And if he did go out, it was because we were dragging him on his leash. All the while, *my* dog was just happy to have a home, sitting out there in the backyard, lying in the sun, like *normal* dogs are supposed to do.

It wasn't long before the new couch wasn't good enough either, and my wife's dog developed a fear of sleeping alone. Once allowed in our bedroom, the conniving little mutt would settle on a soft patch of carpet and snore all night, waking occasionally to lick himself just loud enough to wake me, but not my deep-sleeping wife. As soon as the dog was sure I was awake, he'd drift off again, undoubtedly having nightmares of being an outdoor dog.

And for a while, he seemed happy. Unfortunately, he soon developed a fear of the space under our bed. God only knows what he thought was under there, probably a doghouse and some generic kibbles, but he would stare and whimper and growl until my wife invited him up *onto* the bed. And there he would lie, legs up in the air, snoring away, right between my wife and me, making sleep nearly impossible. For me. It's difficult to keep the spark alive in any marriage, even without a drooling, fifty-pound, furry baby lying between you. Meanwhile, *my* dear sweet dog

## The Pampered Pooch

was still lying out back in the carpeted handcrafted doghouse I'd built for the infiltrator.

A short time after my wife's dog had become a fixture in the bedroom he had the gall to go on a hunger strike, boycotting his economy-brand dog food. At first he'd just throw it up, usually on the carpet he wouldn't sleep on. But then he just plain refused to eat it. My wife said he was allergic to the cheap ingredients, so after buying three different brands of kibbles, he finally settled on the most expensive one hundred percent chicken and beef brand.

Meanwhile, as the prima donna slept in a soft bed and supped on victuals fit for a king, my poor dog slept out back, slowly eating the year's supply of cheap dog food that I'd recently acquired.

Over several months, the pooch prince conveniently developed a fear of loud noises, most particularly my voice. Every time I yelled, he would piddle on the floor like a puppy, so my wife made me stop yelling at him. As luck would have it, a thunderstorm hit in the wee hours of Easter morning, and needless to say, the mangy mutt was deathly afraid of lightning and thunder. So much so that he whined and cried the whole night through. Following our basket-toting eldest daughter out to the living room the next morning, she stopped dead in her tracks and said, "What's that?"

Following her finger, we were disgusted to see a giant mound of dog doo, right smack dab in the middle of our living room floor. I don't know if it was the lightning, the thunder, or that new bag of all-protein dog chow with the real beef gravy, but I immediately glared at my wife, and then at *her* dog, who sheepishly slinked off in the other direction. We would have just cleaned it up if our two-year-old hadn't come flying down the hall in a full sprint headed straight for the Easter doo dropping.

Leaping towards the baby, as much to save the carpets as anything, my quick-thinking wife said, "Oh, watch out kids, it looks like the Easter Bunny left more than eggs this year."

Aghast, I was unable to believe she'd uttered such a thing, but the kids thought that was the best thing they'd ever heard … or seen … or nearly stepped in. That was all the proof they'd ever need. In fact, they were determined to get up a little earlier next year, just to catch a glimpse of the Easter Bunny in action.

I tried to stay mad at my wife's dog, but watching the magical wonder in a child's face at Easter or Christmas is one of the purest joys a person can experience. The seven-year-old, wise beyond her years, was already growing incredulous: Why does a bunny lay eggs? How does Santa get in without a chimney?

We figured we'd bought at least two more years of make-believe, just from that big ol' bunny's indiscretion. Heck, if we can get Rudolph to take a pee on the Christmas tree this year, we should be able to keep the magic alive through high school.

# Trash Day: The Need to Belong

When my wife and I and our two young daughters moved into a small home on the Central Oregon Coast, we had no idea a band of cutthroat marauders had been terrorizing the neighborhood for well over a year. Attacking by cover of night, while the simple folk of Seal Rock slept, their ruthlessness was only outweighed by their complete lack of contrition. Their ringleader, a one-eyed albino named Pinky, was particularly shameless, and he had become the scourge of every man, woman, and child on our street.

Just before he drove away, the house's previous owner reminded us to put our trash receptacle out on Thursday evenings because the garbage truck comes early on Friday.

We slept soundly that first Thursday night, proud new homeowners. Sadly, our joy was short-lived, because when I emerged Friday morning I was mortified to discover my trash receptacle had been toppled and its contents laid bare for all the world to see. I felt so naked and ashamed, but to my great relief, as I glanced up and down my street, there

## The Unnatural Aging of Cheese

were toppled cans, like giant green dominoes, as far as the eye could see. My newfound friends all came to my aide.

"Damn, raccoons!" they said. They told me not to worry, that it happened to everyone. We felt the depth of each other's pain and we bonded there that first Friday morning. For the first time in my life, I felt I *belonged* somewhere. I was ... a *neighbor*!

The following week passed quickly and on Thursday evening I wheeled out my can again. When I awoke on Friday I was expecting the worst, but was delighted to find my can standing perfectly erect and untouched, like a gleaming green pillar of refuse. A quick glance up the street revealed that my neighbors had not fared so well.

Now, misery loves company, and as I watched each one of my new friends emerge to their private mess, I was sure I saw a hint of resentment in their eyes. And so it came to be, week after week, as my can went unscathed, I became more and more ostracized from the group.

I began to dread Friday mornings. Weaving in and out of their debris fields on my way to work, I could feel their hot envious glares upon me. I could nearly hear their whispers, just out of earshot, speculating as to what sort of unholy magic I had employed to keep those barbarous beasts at bay.

Finally, I could take it no longer. Humans are communal creatures after all, with a visceral need to belong. So, as crazy as it sounds, I set about sneaking out in the wee hours of the morning, hoping to facilitate the pillaging of my own garbage by those persnickety pests. I began by removing the

## Trash Day: The Need to Belong

bungee cords, and when that failed, I flipped the lid back to allow them easier entry. Next I tried sprinkling a little trash around my can just to wet their palettes for waste, like a little refuse appetizer. As week after week passed and nothing seemed to work, I became more desperate, eventually tipping my can over and making a trail of garbage to my nearest neighbor. And with each successive failure, my desperation grew.

The following Thursday night, in a last-ditch effort, I set out my receptacle with a particularly alluring trail of extra creamy peanut butter, and then I climbed onto my roof to wait.

About a quarter past five, Pinky and his band of mischievous miscreants came marching single file down my street, toppling cans and setting off floodlights with absolute impunity. They were clearly enjoying the endless procession of driveway buffets and they were headed straight for me. But when they reached my property line, as God is my witness, those self-righteous, sanctimonious little scavengers actually crossed the street, and upon reaching the other end of my property, they crossed back again and continued their feasting next door. I was incensed, I tell you.

Unable to swallow this final indignity, I descended from my roof, sprinted down the driveway and, reaching into my can, picked up a particularly unsavory and overcooked twelve-ounce t-bone my wife had ruined the night before. As the sun began to break over the horizon, I flung it at Pinky with every drop of strength I could muster. His pals scattered as if they had seen the devil himself. A short while

## The Unnatural Aging of Cheese

later, when he regained consciousness and his one pink eye fell upon what had struck him, both his little eyebrows raised up in a sort of shocked horror. He turned tail and beat feet across my neighbor's lawn, over his fence, and into the forest from whence he'd come. At that point, I fell to my knees and sobbed, overcome with loneliness and faced with the prospect of having to move.

Just as I thought all hope was lost, a bright ray of sun came shining down my street and all at once I was suffused in the glow of total enlightenment. When you love someone, you must sometimes withhold the truth in order to protect them. As I might have mentioned, my wife, unbeknownst to her, is quite possibly the worst cook on earth, but most certainly the worst cook west of the Mississippi, and almost assuredly the worst cook in the entire contiguous United States. In our family, we exchange Heimlich maneuvers like hugs, and Pepto-Bismol is an after-dinner liqueur. The few insipid dishes that manage to reach one's stomach are usually so dry and overcooked that they must be chased with prodigious amounts of liquid to prevent the entire digestive track from seizing up.

I had assumed that carrion-eating creatures would dance a celebratory cha-cha-cha at finding a sun-baked bit of road kill, but clearly I was wrong. And that's when the solution hit me—so simple it was hard to believe I hadn't seen it from the start.

On Thursday evenings now, there comes a quiet knock at my back door and after my wife goes off to watch Jeopardy, my daughter and I open our Raccoon Repulsion Service.

## Trash Day: The Need to Belong

The neighbors know to line up single file and to have exact change. There's no need for a price list: the fee is five dollars for a side dish and ten for a main entrée. Just place the item on top of your receptacle and you're guaranteed to never see a raccoon again. Amazingly, it also works on bears, badgers and Africanized bees. According to reports, Pinky and the gang have been terrorizing the next subdivision over, so we're looking at expanding. Sometimes I feel a little guilty, like maybe I should tell them that the side dishes have the same powers of repulsion as the main entrees, but it's a perceived value so who am I to judge?

Yes, I considered buying my wife cooking lessons as a present, but I just don't have the heart to tell her how bad she is. And besides, I've been able to pay off one of our vehicles and squirrel away a little for the kids' college education. Besides, what she doesn't know won't hurt her. And, as long as we don't eat those things, they won't hurt us either.

# The Dousing of Mr. Dingles

**Sure, scrubbing your cat's butt** sounds easy enough, in theory. However, trust me when I tell you it is anything but. In addition to their well-known aversion to water, cats are not particularly fond of having their butts touched. Unfortunately, you don't know these things until you actually try, but my wounds have healed now and if this harrowing account can help one person scrub their cat's butt safely, then it will have been well worth it.

Personally, I don't really like cats, but I was outnumbered by my wife and elder daughter, so against my better judgment, Sir Albert Francis Dingles III was officially inducted into our family in the fall of 2003. For expediency's sake, he quickly became known as Mr. Dingles.

I kid you not, less than a year after his arrival, that disdainful and haughty creature had usurped all my power and deposed me as the ruler of my own home. Not to mention stealing my family's affections, and worst of all, my spot on the couch. The cat grew into an enormous white fur ball, and when he wasn't actually gorging himself, he could

# The Dousing of Mr. Dingles

be found taking a siesta somewhere comfy in the house. The closest that cat came to catching a mouse was the time he helped himself to a brick of cheddar cheese and then fell asleep with his mouth open. I've known some lazy cats in my time, but Mr. Dingles was truly a waste of some perfectly good fur and claws.

One day last fall, hearing a familiar scratching, I pulled open the door and Mr. Dingles went staggering towards his water dish like a drunken sailor. His fur was uncharacteristically unkempt and something about him just seemed off. As he stood there lapping insatiably, I couldn't help but notice that he was covered with what appeared be crusty brown mud, from his tail tip to the bottoms of his hind feet. As I approached from behind, a rank tsunami of stink overcame me, nearly causing me to revisit my lunch. Just when I thought things could get no worse, Mr. Dingles let off five audible cat farts, which are really quite rare, so I knew something was seriously wrong.

Afraid of the truth, but needing to confirm my worst fears, I scooped Dingles under his belly and cautiously went in for a sniff. What happened next is really too graphic to tell, but my cat suffered an abrupt depressurization. I don't know if it was intentional, or if I squeezed his bloated abdomen too tight, but as we drew eye-to-eye, so to speak, I was unprepared for feline flatus of that magnitude. I felt my gag reflex kick in, and it was all I could do to keep from retching. For over a year that cat had strutted around my home like his you-know-what didn't stink, and I am here to tell you, friend, it most certainly did.

# The Unnatural Aging of Cheese

Although not formally trained as a vulcanologist, I surmised that Mr. Dingles, a known glutton, had gobbled up a prodigious amount of something undesirable and it had passed through his system at a high rate of speed, then violently erupted from his hind end. And like a mini-Mount St. Helens, the poopy pyroclastic blast that ensued had matted his fur in a concentric pattern, leaving behind a crusty brown residue from tail tip to toes.

Absolutely disgusted, I extended him out from my body as far as humanly possible, and screamed for my wife.

Racing into the room, she grimaced and glared disapprovingly at me, but I assured her it had been the cat this time. As she opened the door, I toted Mr. Dingles out back, where I set him down on the deck and took a much-needed breath of fresh air. Clearly, the cat needed a bath, but having never washed a cat before, we were somewhat unfamiliar with proper cat-cleansing techniques. Obviously, logic dictated we would need a cleanser of some sort and a water source, so my quick-thinking wife grabbed the dog shampoo and a garden hose. Meanwhile, I pushed the queasy kitty over on one side and proceeded to grab him around both sets of ankles. Lifting him up and extending him out over the porch railing, Mr. Dingles' expression moved from one of confusion to concern. However, his attention was quickly diverted when my wife began squirting a torrent of icy water into his blustery backside.

Not surprisingly, Mr. Dingles withstood this humiliation for slightly less than one second before fully extending his claws and exposing his pointed fangs in a way that

## The Dousing of Mr. Dingles

seemed to indicate he was going to gnaw off one or more of my fingers. It was only by a combination of unnatural contortions and the use of centrifugal force that I managed to keep my digits out of harm's way. Fearing an eventual loss of flesh, I immediately yelled for my wife to cease and desist from our current course of treatment.

Mr. Dingles relaxed a bit, thinking that he'd won the war, but he underestimated our resourcefulness. I quickly contrived a new and improved plan that would ensure the safety of my flesh but, more importantly, leave his bottom spotless. He watched with what one could describe only as a morbid curiosity as my wife returned from the garage with a broom and some duct tape. I don't know if a cat can think, "What in the Sam Hill?" but he certainly had that perplexed expression on his little white face.

As I slowly inched my hands down his struggling appendages, Mr. Dingles must have sensed something because he started craning his neck and gnashing his teeth. He seemed to settle down once his paws were all taped together, and then we simply slipped the broomstick through his legs and I lifted him up and out over the railing, like a fluffy white pig on a spit.

With the safety of our new contrivance, we commenced the cleansing process once more. This time, I held the shampoo in one hand and the broomstick in the other. I had the broom bristles firmly clamped under my arm while my wife squirted water with her left hand and reluctantly scrubbed our cat's tuchas with her right. And all the while, Mr. Dingles, that big baby, carried on like we were pulling out his whiskers. He let loose with a burst of yowls and hisses that one might only hear during an alley cat melee.

The job was certainly unpleasant, but we took pride in our work and we were making good progress. We stopped momentarily just once, when I mistakenly criticized her washing style. It was at that point that she said she would gladly hold the broom if I cared to scrub the cat's butt. Thanking her for the kind offer, I assured her she was doing a fine job, told her how much I respected her as a person, and we continued.

I don't rightly know if the water pressure propelled Mr. Dingles forward, or if it was his constant attempts to shimmy away from the chilly torrent, but whichever it was, that waterlogged kitty inched past the balance point of the broomstick and I was unable to counter-balance him with only one hand. So the broomstick dipped about forty-five degrees, and good ol' Mr. Dingles went sliding right off the end. He sort of hovered there in mid-air for a moment, at which point he looked back at me with this woeful, why-hast-thou-forsaken-me look, which made even a cat-hater like myself feel a little bad. Sort of.

Surprisingly, that myth about cats always landing on their feet and having good balance—well, it's true—because Mr. Dingles landed perfectly upright in that dark brown mud puddle below. And he would have stayed upright if not for that little inconvenience of his little paws being all taped together. So he just kind of teetered there for a second or two, and then tipped over onto one side with a splash. Fearing for his safety, we jumped down off the porch and

## The Dousing of Mr. Dingles

snatched him up out of the muck. As you might imagine, Mr. Dingles looked something like an Oreo cookie with one side peeled off. Unfortunately, I think that final indignity was just a little more than he could stand because his eyes kind of glazed over and he seemed to take on a distant stare. Some might call it catatonia, no pun intended.

At that point, my wife looked concerned. She was clearly having second thoughts. I assured her that Mr. Dingles was still breathing, and so we threaded him back onto the spit and hung him back out there again, making darn sure to tape him to the broomstick this time.

Her fears were quickly allayed, because the second the cold water hit Mr. Dingles his glassy-eyed look was gone and he was madder than hell all over again. Talk about overreacting. He was yeering and yowling so much that the neighbors on both sides came to their windows, no doubt wondering what we were doing to the poor creature. There's nothing worse than nosy neighbors, but there was no way we were stopping. We were *that* close to being done.

Throwing the stick over my shoulder like a hobo, I took Mr. Dingles to dry a patch of ground, laid him down, and cut him free.

I'd be lying to say I wasn't somewhat concerned that the cat might try to exact revenge, but to my great relief, Mr. Dingles just took off like a flash, through the yard and up and over our eight-foot fence, looking back only once to make sure I wasn't following him. Clearly I had been wrong about him not being fast. It appeared he had merely lacked motivation. My wife asked if I thought he'd come back and I told her I didn't rightly know, but at least he'd be clean if he did.

A short time later, an officer from the Humane Society showed up and interrogated me for nearly three hours. It seems there were a couple anonymous reports of alleged animal cruelty. Anonymous and erroneous, I might add. No doubt, if it had been their cat, they would have done the same thing.

As it turns out, a few bits of fur-covered duct tape and a clawed up fence are not evidence of a crime, and with no victim to speak of, I was released on my own recognizance. Anyway, everyone knows eyewitness testimony is highly unreliable.

When Mr. Dingles did not come home that night, my wife and elder daughter were nothing short of distraught. The next afternoon they posted flyers around our neighborhood, bemoaning their loss and beseeching someone to find their beloved little kitty and bring him home. They even offered a $50 reward for his safe return, which I thought was about $50 more than Mr. Dingles was worth. My suggestion of adding the words, "dead or alive," was not received well, and my wife suggested I keep my true feelings to myself, particularly because an impressionable child was involved. So, I just bit my lip and savored my Dingles-less existence.

Unfortunately, three days later, there came a familiar scratching at the door, and like Lazarus returning from the dead, my wife pulled it open. There sat Mr. Dingles himself, in all his gleaming white glory. Trying to hide my surprise, I

## The Dousing of Mr. Dingles

watched through the corner of my eye as he strutted across the foyer and headed for the kitchen. When he halted halfway and turned towards me, our eyes met. The tension could be cut with a knife.

Mr. Dingles must have sensed my fear, because the big cat charged and came at me like a roaring bundle of feline fury. There I sat, unarmed and defenseless with hardly a moment to spare. But quickly grabbing a lavender throw pillow and the universal remote control, I readied myself for battle.

Mr. Dingles closed in on me, and just as I was drawing back to strike him a good one—on the top of his head—he halted dead in his tracks. Stretching out his two front legs in a form of feline bow, he leapt into my lap, where he curled into a fluffy white ball and began to purr. At first I was afraid to touch him, thinking it a trick, but I soon came to realize that the mighty cat had been tamed. I don't know if we stumbled onto some form of humiliation-obedience training or what, but Mr. Dingles was most certainly a changed kitty. From that day forward, he would await my arrival by the front door and, after following me in, would sit patiently while I took my rightful place on the couch. Only when I was settled would he jump into my lap, curling up for a snooze.

Believe it or not, I actually began to enjoy this daily ritual, but Lord knows there's nothing worse than a flip-flopper, so I'd usually wait for my wife and children to leave the room before petting him.

Twice a month, unbeknownst to them, I started taking

# The Unnatural Aging of Cheese

Mr. Dingles to the Boo Boo Kitty Boutique down on Main Street for a private grooming. After all, he does represent our family and therefore needs to look his very best. I bought him one of those super-deluxe multi-tiered climbing structures. It's the fully carpeted kind that features two retractable rope swings and an automated nip dispenser. The darn thing takes up half the living room, but we needed a smaller entertainment center anyways.

This past December, Lady Elizabeth Jillian Sinclair joined our family. She and Mr. Dingles became fast friends and were wed in February in a ceremony performed by my daughter on the deck of the two-bedroom kitty condo I built in the old maple out back. The neighbors thought we'd overdone it, but the little tux and gown didn't really cost all that much. And they looked so cute! We even bronzed his little top hat for posterity's sake. You should have seen them climb the condo steps together, nuzzle, and then exchange matching flea collars. It was really quite touching.

I've no idea how long the gestation period of a cat is, but my wife says they're going to name one of the kittens after me. A little cute fluffy one, I hope.

# A Brush with Death

During a recent near-death experience, while scrambling to paint the exterior of my house before the winter rains, I became acutely aware of just how little value my family places on my survival. Now, admittedly, I should have painted the house over the summer, but it's hard to find time in today's busy world, what with twenty-four-hour sports networks and the invention of ice-cold beer. And, in my defense, as soon as I saw the Portland weatherman call for seven glorious days of Indian summer, I got right out there on the sixth day and started taping off the house.

I had never so much as painted a birdhouse before and, to my great surprise, it is far more difficult than one might think. Just for some frame of reference, if you're not a house painter either, it takes about six beers to tape off a small ranch-style home (eight if you paint the gutters). And when you factor in two naps and a snack break, you must really budget your time wisely. This left just day seven for the actual painting.

# The Unnatural Aging of Cheese

To tell the truth, we did not do a lot of painting growing up in my family, as we were upper-middle class, not exactly rich (but we sure acted like it). Some might even say I was born with a silver spork in my mouth, but I'll have you know that I am a moderately hardworking, God-fearing American. One who loosely models himself after the Lord. But, whereas, He made the world in six days and rested on the seventh, I tend to rest for the first six and hop right to it on the seventh. In all fairness, and I'm sure you'll agree, the Lord is a tough act to follow.

This may sound slightly paranoid, but I'd noticed for some time that my two young daughters like their mother best. As did our two dogs (even the one I picked out), both cats (not that I cared), and, as odd as it sounds, even my eldest daughter's goldfish seemed to flip me the fin during feedings. I tried not to take it personally, or read too much into it, but nobody cried when Dad left, nobody cheered when Dad came home. It was always Momma this, and Momma that. Spontaneous declarations of "We love Momma!" and "We miss Momma!" Yada yada yada. It was enough to give a man an inferiority complex.

There I was, perched precariously on the top step of my eight-foot ladder, performing the thankless and unceremonious job of painting my house's exterior. Meanwhile that unappreciative group of interlopers was enjoying itself inside *my* home. All the while I was painting, my neighbor on the east, Ned—who fancies himself a jack-of-all-trades—was yapping away with his pointless commentary, saying things like, "Sure looks like rains a'comin'," and "You know

## A Brush with Death

that warnin' label there says not to stand above the seven foot level," and so on and what not. I tell you, I just wanted to say, "Shut the hell up, Ned, and mind your own damn business." But Ned never was one to take a hint. And I had noticed that when he wasn't busy running his mouth and being a know-it-all, he was flitting about the neighborhood spreading scuttlebutt.

So, finally, when he told me not to lean *my own* ladder against the side of *my own* house, suggesting instead that I extend the legs to provide a more stable base upon which to stand, I had had enough. I tersely thanked him for his unneeded advice and assured him that I had been painting houses since *long* before he had arrived home that day, and that I had a pretty darn good idea what I was doing. And then I zapped Ned with an evil eye that my Aunt Mable had taught me just before she was blinded in an unfortunate fly-fishing accident, and mercifully that chased Ned right back into his own garage where he belonged. Finally, I had some peace and quiet in which to work.

Okay, so I live in a one-story ranch home, but I've never cared much for heights and I must admit that the apex of that roof seemed a heck of lot higher than it appeared from the ground. And so as I stood there, straining to extend that brush up as high as it would go, I felt this odd sort of a shimmy, or one might say a shake, and it sort of rippled, or reverberated, throughout my body, from the tips of my outstretched fingers down to the tippy-toes I was standing on. And unfortunately, that shimmy continued right on through the ladder as well. And it was shortly thereafter that my

## The Unnatural Aging of Cheese

brain realized something was horribly wrong and it was at that point that I started flapping my arms uncontrollably like a bird or a tightrope walker, at which point I made the fatal mistake of all high-wire performers: I glanced down. From my mind's eye, it seemed like I was standing on the Empire State Building. I felt the blood run out of my face, taking along with it all my confidence and sense of well-being.

At the risk of sounding arrogant, I am somewhat of an athlete, and I do believe my body is my temple. *But ...* let's just say my temple, much like the exterior of my home, had fallen into some minor level of disrepair these past few years. Not irreparable, mind you, just a little weathered. I think the real estate term is "suffering from deferred maintenance." That said, eight feet seemed like a long way for me and my two-hundred-fifty-pound temple to drop, considering all that deferred maintenance I was suffering from. Anyhow, as so often happens, just when all hope is lost, opportunity seems to present itself, and my salvation came in the form of a seven-foot weather-beaten fence, in dire need of some stain.

You see, once that ladder finally decided which way we were going to fall and I saw that fence coming at me, I quickly formulated Plan C, which I felt extremely confident would save me. For your information, Plan A had been the uncontrollable flapping, and Plan B had been a valiant effort to dig my fingernails into the siding as we went down flush with the wall. Plan B had, surprisingly, yielded only mixed results. So, there I was, just me and Plan C, heading straight for the top of the fence.

## A Brush with Death

Plan C, as you might have guessed, was to land my right foot on top of the fence while keeping my left foot planted safely on top of the ladder, leaving me spread-eagled in mid-air, forming an enormous upside-down letter "Y."

Plan C had sounded pretty good in theory but, in my defense, after Plans A and B failed so unexpectedly, I hadn't had much time to think it through. I'm not sure what exactly I would have done had Plan C worked, leaving me stuck in a spread-eagle stance, but it didn't work, so that is neither here nor there. Oh, Plan C wasn't an absolute failure. It started out just fine. And my right foot hit the fence exactly where I aimed it, right in the crux between the horizontal wood crossbeam and the vertical wooden planks. But who knew that, after just half of one second and a momentary false sense of security, those planks would give way, forcing me to leap from the ladder and land crotch first atop the fence's crossbeam in the plankless gap I had just created. There I was, snugly pinched on both sides by the remaining planks, suspended some six feet above the ground. And worse yet, the displaced planks were still attached at the bottom, now angling out ominously at about 45 degrees, like a great crocodile jaw. Their rusty tetanus-covered nails protruded like giant teeth, just inches from my right thigh. So there I dangled on that four-inch crossbeam like a big fat gymnast straddling a balance beam or a cowboy glued to his horse. I was trapped by my own enormous girth and I was wincing in pain.

My crashing into the fence had made a good deal of racket and I may have even screamed a little, but to my

## The Unnatural Aging of Cheese

great dismay, did my family come running out to see if I was okay? No, they did not. Why, they were inside, eating crab cakes and enjoying themselves in the safety and comfort of *my* home! I was helplessly stranded, rusty nails just inches from a major artery, and did they wonder why I was still screaming? No, they didn't even care enough to check it out, but of course, that nitwit neighbor, Ned, came running.

"You okay? I heard a crash! You need help, neighbor?"

"I'm fine, Ned," I lied.

"Are you sure? That sounded painful!"

"Ned, clearly you haven't painted in a while. Can't you see I'm just trying to paint this tough spot above the fence?"

"Well then, why's your paintbrush lyin' in the driveway?"

Frustrated, I screamed, "Ned, I'm fine, damn it! Just leave me alone!"

But in his usual nosy Ned fashion, he just stood there watching as I tried in vain to lift my own body weight and pull my right foot up onto the crossbeam. Every time I would get close, though, arms shaking uncontrollably with the strain, my pant leg or shoelace would snag on those damn crocodile teeth, and I would collapse back down, hyperventilating and exhausted. After three humiliating attempts at this, Ned said he was going to go call for help, at which point I screamed, "NOOOO!" and using my last ounce of strength and dignity, I started tipping myself over until my inside foot touched the semi-detached planks. I pushed off with all my might, detaching them the rest of way, but thankfully generating enough thrust to clear the

## A Brush with Death

crossbeam and land headlong in my un-watered and weed-filled flower garden.

And, as I lay there, covered in dirt and fertilizer, head and shoulders throbbing and trying desperately to catch my wind, I thought about all the different paths my life could have taken and how I had ended up there. As I climbed to my feet, dusted myself off, and started limping towards the back door and my miserable unappreciated existence beyond, the back door suddenly snapped open and my two prized black labs came bounding out, headed straight for me. And as our eyes met, their excitement was palpable and there was a definite moment between us. All at once, I knew that I was loved, and that life was not nearly so bad after all.

And as they ran right past me, jumped through the new hole I'd just punched in the fence, and took off down the street, I thought to myself, *Now ain't that a bitch?*

# Black Friday: Operation Shop and Awe

Friend, I am fresh from the field of battle, and I hope you never have to bear witness to the things I've just seen. Trust me when I say it is hell out there, particularly this modern day consumer warfare. Greed is the root of all evil, and there is nothing sadder than seeing friend versus friend, and neighbor versus neighbor, engaged in a ruthless war over meaningless turf and material possessions. Well, nothing sadder except the retailers and media hype igniting such a consumer conflagration the day after a day of thanksgiving. I don't know, but it seems immoral. I am a red-blooded American capitalist, but I have now served Uncle Sam Walton once and would refuse to fight if ever called again.

On November 25, 2005, upon entering what was once my kitchen, I was confronted by a small but tough-looking army sergeant who bore a striking resemblance to a woman I once called my wife. Trust me when I say this sergeant was mean as the day is long, her powers of persuasion unparalleled,

## Black Friday: Operation Shop and Awe

and her silver-tongued recruiting methods nearly impossible to resist. She assured me that all my material dreams were within my grasp, and most for an irresistible one-third to one-half off. She then asked if I was willing to follow her into battle. When I showed a hint of reservation, she questioned my patriotism and asked me how I could consider myself a *true* American. She told me that this is a consumer society and that my freedom to over-consume is not free, and that men had died for my right of gluttony.

So naïve was I then, that the next thing I knew my head was bent over the toilet bowl while Sarge shaved it with a pair of dog-grooming shears.

Boot camp is a living hell, I tell you. Sarge turned our living room into a military-style obstacle course and I was forced to climb over the couch, crawl under the coffee table, ramble over the love seat, and then remain concealed in our fireplace for what seemed like hours. Day and night, leading up to my deployment, she would march me around the house as I sounded off, "Shopping is my goal in life; I take orders from my wife! Left, left, left-right, left!"

Pointing out common household objects, she would bark, "Seize it, Soldier," and if I failed to take hold in what she deemed a reasonable amount of time, she'd dress me down, demanding push-ups and sit-ups, which greatly amused our children. When I objected, she told me I was a flabby, good-for-nothing and that I'd better believe the enemy was not so soft. She said the enemy was lean and mean, and willing to train harder, so that they could wrest those savings from my very own pocket.

## The Unnatural Aging of Cheese

Just after Thanksgiving dinner, which I was too tired to enjoy, I received my first marching orders. We were due to ship out the next morning and I was to report to the front door at 0400. Sarge saw my concern and tried to quell my nerves with shopping war stories from The Wally War and The Macy's Day Massacre, where she'd received two Purple Carts and a Concessional Medal of Honor. It did not help, however.

Nervous about the coming conflict, I was unable to sleep most of that night. Bleary-eyed and yawning, I arrived at the front door as instructed, and Sarge rubbed grease paint all over my face. As I drove our gas guzzling SUV at breakneck speed, she drilled me on battle tactics and reminded me of my oath of service. When I answered incorrectly, she'd order me to pull over immediately and question my toughness. She'd ask if I wanted to quit, and I would blubber in Richard Gere-ish fashion, "Sir, no, sir! I got nowhere else to go! Sir!"

To Sarge's great chagrin, we didn't hit Wally World until well after 0500, and by that time the battlefield was already littered with enemy vehicles, empty artillery carts, and wounded soldiers from the front. As I exited our vehicle, a retreating soldier ran up and told me it was hell in there, and if I knew what was good for me, I'd run away from Sarge and never look back.

In hindsight, I wish I'd heeded his advice, but what Sarge lacks in size, she makes up for in emotional intimidation, so I went around back and started unloading our gear.

Sarge took point as we snuck up to the front door. She

## Black Friday: Operation Shop and Awe

ordered me to cover our flank and to make sure we hadn't been followed.

Somehow Sarge commandeered a squeaky-wheeled cart from a blue-vested friendly and we headed off towards electronics. It did not take me long to realize that there is no honor among combat shoppers. It is truly every man, woman, and child for themselves. As a big man, I thought I might have some slight advantage, but I soon realized that it is the small and the quick that prosper in consumer warfare. In my defense, the old man who snatched the last self-cleaning nose hair clippers from my hand was much quicker than he appeared, walker or no walker. Regardless of his unnatural spryness, a zero for 1 start quickly brought Sarge's wrath. She dressed me down publicly for forgetting the first rule of combat shopping: never underestimate the enemy, and never, ever, under any circumstances, was I to actually look at the item I wanted to buy.

Next we were off to the dreaded toy department, tougher to navigate than a Viet Cong minefield. Sarge scrutinized the map and it appeared to be just eight aisles, or clicks as she referred to them, from of our current position. Agreeing to rendezvous in toys at 0600, we synchronized our watches and headed out on two side missions. I successfully captured a George Foreman Grill in Home & Appliance, and Sarge secured a Chenille bath rug from Bed & Bath. We both arrived in Toys at precisely 0600.

To our great dismay, the toy aisle had been ravaged, but as we started to wheel away, Sarge spotted a much-coveted three-foot stuffed Dora the Explorer doll, and yelled, "Seize it, Soldier!" I reached for Dora's arm, and as luck would have it, a golden-curled five-year old grabbed hold of her leg. Unsure what to do in the event of a tie, I looked back at Sarge, who mimicked a violent yanking motion. However, as I peered into that poor girl's innocent face, I just didn't have the heart to tear a stuffed doll from her grasp. Fortunately, the centrifugal force from our spinning sent her careening off into a twelve-foot cage of lightweight fluorescent balls, which scattered in every direction, and thankfully broke her fall. Sarge quickly ascertained that I felt a little sorry for the girl, but quickly slapped me across the face, told me to snap back to my senses, and said there was no place for empathy in war. Besides, she pointed out, technically the kid had let go, albeit somewhat unwillingly. Sarge ripped the doll out of my hands, threw it in the basket, and told me we needed to leave before the child's commanding officer showed up.

Our final stop was Housewares, where Sarge had been eyeing a lovely twelve-piece set of gold-banded dinnerware for months. According to the advertisement, they were half-off and there was nothing and nobody going to stop her from owning a set. Unfortunately, nothing is exactly what we found on the shelf, and a bunch of nobodies is who she said had stolen her most coveted item. In a last straw-grasping measure, Sarge stopped a procurement clerk, but as expected, he said the supply depot was barren. Ultimately, we had won a few battles but lost the war, and Sarge took it pretty hard. I actually felt bad for her, for a moment.

Sarge spotted the silver-haired old woman rounding the corner with what must have been the last box of twelve-

## Black Friday: Operation Shop and Awe

piece gold-banded dinnerware in Oregon tucked neatly in the shelf under the basket of her cart. The woman appeared to be traveling alone and headed towards checkout, so Sarge said time was of the essence. Following her orders, I went off to flank the old woman, while Sarge took our cart and raced double-time down the center aisle to lay in wait.

As the old woman went rolling by, Sarge raced out and slammed into her cart, spilling the box of gold-banded dinnerware onto the floor. While she diverted the old woman's attention with an insincere apology, I crawled out on my belly from behind a six-foot pallet of strawberry Slim Fast and slowly made my way towards that prized dinnerware. Periodically glancing up to make sure I hadn't been spotted, I proceeded to hook an arm around that box, then slowly scootched it back towards my hiding place. Personally, I felt a little guilty, but I had to admit that Sarge's plan was working to perfection. I was about to push myself onto all fours when I heard the sound of air being ripped asunder, followed by a thundering thwack, and then I felt a very hard thump on the top of my head. Looking back over my shoulder, the old woman was straddling me with a thirty-six-inch tube of festive wrapping paper raised over her head like Excalibur.

You wouldn't think an old woman could hit that hard, but this old bird must have been a Samurai in a past life because she rained blows down on me from every angle imaginable—thunk, thunk, thunk, thunk. As I would raise an arm to protect my face, the old woman would go for a rib-shot or worse, and when I went to cover my ribs, why, she'd pop me on the head again. Most frightening was the maniacal look in her eyes. As one tube bent, she would just reach over to the aisle display and re-arm herself. I know it sounds crazy, but I became fearful for my life, and terrified at the prospect of being the first person ever beaten to death with a holiday roll of wrapping paper.

Although disoriented, I somehow managed to get to my feet as quick-thinking Sarge threw me the stuffed Dora doll, presumably to defend myself. Not normally one to hit a lady, I saw no other option, and so I gripped Dora's ankles tightly and I whacked that old woman right alongside her head. My mighty blow did not even seem to faze that thick-headed antiquity, but boy did it make her mad when she realized her wig was missing. If given half a chance, I would have gladly retrieved it from that passing man's basket, but that violent old biddy blocked my way, snatched up a four-roll economy pack, and prepared to strike a final deathblow. Call me a coward, but I turned tail and took off running, leaving those God-forsaken dishes lying there on the floor.

The old lady gave me a pretty good chase, but I eventually lost her in Automotive, and then spent the next hour-and-a-half hiding in Home and Garden. Apparently, when she took off after me, Sarge snatched up those dishes and made for the checkout stand, but Granny was not to be outsmarted. Like the Rommel of Retail, she doubled back and caught Sarge red-handed in the express lane. Store security physically removed her from the Wally World premises and she's currently serving a lifetime ban, replete with a backroom mug shot and all. As for me, I was able to escape when the coast cleared, but needless to say, we were unable to purchase any of our items. Sarge gave me a dishonorable discharge, which was just fine by me.

The VA support group has been pretty helpful with my Post Traumatic Shopping Disorder, but I still flinch every time I see a tube of wrapping paper or hear the crinkle of cellophane.

# You Can't Pick Your Sister

As every parent knows, there are moments in a child's upbringing where their behavior is so utterly bizarre that you actually question whether the munchkins are truly your genetic offspring, or perhaps they were switched at birth. My two children are no exception, and although preliminary results have them leaning in my genealogical direction, I am still anxiously awaiting further study.

Like many couples, my wife and I take turns driving our seven-year-old to school and dropping the two-year-old off at childcare. The conversation during these drives, between the two sisters, is sometimes amusing, occasionally disturbing, and quite often both. But it's certainly never boring, as was the case this past Tuesday.

When you're focusing on the road, it's hard to pay complete attention to what's going on in the backseat, but over time you develop a parental ear that locks in on sounds of teasing, touching, slapping, hitting, pinching, poking, jabbing, grabbing, hoarding, and the like. So, as we drove along last Tuesday, my highly attuned ear locked in on my eldest (we've always had to watch that one) as she gave the Little One some unauthorized instructions.

"Step One" she said, "Stick out finger."

My Spidey-sense began to tingle, but curious where this might be leading, I just shot off a warning glance in the rearview mirror. The Little One was watching attentively as the Big One sat with her left index finger pointed toward the sky.

"No, Sis, your other finger," said the Big One.

The Little One, always seeking approval, dropped her pinky and proceeded to raise her index finger.

"Good," the Big One said.

I was cautiously concerned, but strangely intrigued, and therefore not yet ready to intervene.

"Step Two," the Big One said, "Insert finger in nose, like so."

*Oh yes, now I see where this is going*, I thought. Another glance in the mirror revealed the Big One holding her left index finger to the side of her left nostril, giving the illusion of picking her nose. And as the little one began enthusiastically sticking her own finger up her actual nostril, I realized it was time to step in.

"No, no, no, no, no," I said, "not funny, guys."

Actually, it was mildly funny, having never witnessed a nose-picking tutorial, but the last thing the Big One needed was encouragement. "Please don't do that," I said. "Not funny."

Clearly pleased with her handy work, the Big One completely ignored me and said, "Step Three. Wiggle finger tip,

## The Unnatural Aging of Cheese

like so." Pulling her index finger down and out, making it appear as if it had come from her nostril, she proceeded to wiggle the tip back and forth in demonstration.

*Oh boy*, I thought, *here we go*. They both giggled and the Little One did as instructed.

"Okay, guys, that's enough. *Not funny*. Fingers away from noses NOW! I mean it! I know you can hear me."

"Step Four," the Big One said.

"No! No Step Four," I said.

"Step Four," the Big One repeated, "pull booger out."

"NO STEP FOUR!" I shouted. But it was too late. The Little One withdrew her finger, and there, resting ever so delicately on the tip, was the daintiest little booger you ever did see. Staring proudly at her unexpected prize, the Little One's grin widened, her eyes lit up with elation as she turned to her sister, who was beaming with pride, and they both began to giggle and snort, which soon erupted into uncontrollable laughter. And I'm embarrassed to admit it, but it *was* pretty funny. As a responsible adult, I tried to control myself, but their laughter was infectious. And the harder I laughed, the harder they laughed, and vice versa, until we were all in hysterics and had tears streaming down our faces. And all was well with the world.

"Step Five," I heard the Big One say.

"Oh, no! No, no, no, no, no, no. ABSOLUTELY NO STEP FIVE!" I boomed.

"Step Five," the Big One repeated.

"I'm not kidding, Big Girl. It's not funny," I said. But, unfortunately, I had just shown it was quite amusing, and paying no attention to me, the Little One awaited her big sister's instructions.

"Eat ...," the Big One said.

"NO! Please no eat! Please no eat," I pleaded.

"Eat...," the Big One repeated, pausing either for dramatic effect or to allow her father to turn the proper shade of red.

"BOOGER!" she bellowed.

"NOOOOOOOOO!" I yelled, turning to see the little one happily obeying.

In a moment of adrenaline-driven hyper-drive that only a parent can truly understand, my hand darted back there like the head of a striking cobra, and grabbing that little forearm, I snatched that booger-tipped finger back just after it had crossed her toothy grin, but just prior to consumption. Breathing a deep sigh of relief, I adjusted my mirror and gave the Big Girl a *very* disapproving look. There she sat, looking proudly defiant, and clearly not concerned about the punishment to follow.

"You, Big Girl," I said, "are in BIG BIG TROUBLE." In my most stern voice I said, "I told you not to do that and you went ahead and did it anyway. Now you'll just have to deal with the consequences."

"I'm sorry," she murmured.

"What?" I asked.

"I'm sorry," she repeated, louder this time.

"Sorry for what?" I asked.

"Sorry for telling, Little Sis to eat her booger," she replied, contritely.

## The Unnatural Aging of Cheese

"And what could you do differently *next time*?" I asked.

She paused a moment, clearly giving thought to the question I'd posed. As her sweet little face turned up and met my stare in the mirror, I felt encouraged that I had actually raised a thoughtful, caring and introspective child.

"Umm, tell her to wipe it on the back of the seat?"

# McVooDoo

**A**dmittedly, **my children have never been** what you'd call quote-unquote *normal*. I'm not one to spook easily, but their behavior, at times, particularly that of the Big One, falls somewhere between unsettling and downright disturbing. Until this most recent incident, however, it did not seem to warrant upsetting their mother.

Odd things had been happening for some time. Over the past year, I'd started noticing items missing from my desk at work, and it seemed to always coincide with my wife bringing the children by the office. It's important for a parent to avoid showing favoritism, but my eldest, the seven-year-old, was most definitely the prime suspect, not to say that her shifty-eyed two-year old sister was above suspicion. Hindsight is 20-20, but the first clue should have been my daughters' unnatural fascination with my stapler, Scotch tape dispenser, and paper clip receptacle, and then the subsequent disappearance of those objects. These were just the first in a long line of missing office supplies, but other than a half-eaten Tootsie Pop and a few sticky fingerprints, I had

## The Unnatural Aging of Cheese

no hard evidence and was thus forced to suffer with the maddening mystery.

I honestly believed there might be some other plausible explanation, until this past Saturday when I went crawling in the rear passenger door of my wife's car and was confronted by a most disturbing discovery. In addition to the empty McDonald's bags, which indicated she'd bought them fast food—again—the back seat and floor were littered with sesame seeds, ketchup drips and French-fries too numerous to count. There were two mustard-slathered pickle slices on the armrest and a nearly whole all-beef patty tucked in the magazine holder. But that's not what frightened me, no! As I looked up towards Heaven to ask God, *Why me?* I was confronted by a most unholy abomination, just pinned there to the back of the driver-side headrest.

Using four straightened paperclips, four French fries, and two-and-a-half chicken nuggets, someone, most likely my eldest, had created what can only be described as ... a *McNugget Man*.

One paperclip ran right through McNugget Man's forehead and pinned him firmly to the headrest, while the second ran vertically, like a thin metallic spine. Along the spine, she'd slid a torso nugget followed closely by a once-bitten crescent moon portion of a third nugget, which appeared to form what looked like shorts or underpants. The third and fourth paperclips had been wound around the crude spine and four French fries were threaded on to make arms and legs. The child's creation was really quite ingenious, despite being a horrible waste of food, and she probably

## McVooDoo

would have got off with a just a warning had I not looked a little closer.

One of my impish offspring had drawn a detailed face on that head nugget using my favorite black Sharpie, which I later found lying on the floor missing its cap. This, in and of itself, was not so upsetting, but as I examined McNugget Man's features, I was confronted by the sparsely populated hairline and thick dark uni-brow that had become a signature trademark of every picture she had ever drawn of me. In addition, my business card had been stapled to one arm, and Scotch taped to his chest were two very thin hairs of my exact coloration. I felt a slight chill run up my spine.

Scrutinizing the creature further, I unconsciously patted my belly and realized that the passing years had not been kind, and that the egg-shaped torso nugget was not that far from the mark. And, admittedly, the fries *were* a pretty good representation of my chicken legs, but regardless of what my wife says, my arms are really quite muscular. That said, other than the French fry arms, the crossed eyes, and the single black tooth, this thing bore a striking resemblance to me.

As you might imagine, seeing your likeness made entirely of deep-fried chunks of reconstituted chicken and French-fried potatoes is quite unsettling, and I felt the hair on the back of my neck stand up.

Just when I thought things could get no stranger, I noticed the spears sticking out of my—I mean McNugget Man's—body. Using shafts of dehydrated pasta pilfered from a package I later found under the seat, she had pierced this poor creature through his abdomen, one arm, and a leg. At first it just seemed cruel and unusual, but it soon occurred to me that my acid reflux had been acting up of late, and I had to cancel Tuesday's golf game because of crick in my knee. And furthermore, that very morning, I'd opened the car door with my left hand, because my tennis elbow was bothering me again. And that's when it hit me!

"In the name of all that is holy," I said, "this child is practicing McVoodoo!"

As expected, the seven-year-old denied all responsibility, but she had no good answers for why the undy nugget was a perfect match to her overbite. We interrogated her younger sister, who was most certainly complicit, but her limited language skills and her icy poker face prohibited us from getting much useful information.

Our priest thought we over-reacted a little. He did not even believe it was truly *Black* magic at work, but clearly it's at least the deep-fried golden brown variety.

## Marital Issue #5: Poor Vehicular Hygiene

Look, I fully understand that compromise is a necessary part of any successful marriage, and that you must accept some of your spouse's personal bad habits, much like they accept yours. But, the matrimonial line must be drawn somewhere and poor vehicular hygiene is just plain unacceptable. We have only two vehicles and sometimes we are forced to swap them to accommodate specific priorities. However, my career *requires* a clean car.

Unfortunately, on some occasions—once a week or so—we need to switch cars, and it never fails: when I receive mine back, it's not quite in the shape I expect.

This past Monday was just one such occasion, so on Tuesday morning, with my two daughters in tow, I approached my car with great trepidation. Keeping my head turned, I inserted the key, twisted, and listened for the power locks to release. And then, preferring to rip the proverbial band-aid off, rather than slowly peel it away, I turned and

## The Unnatural Aging of Cheese

quickly thrust my head inside to survey the damage.

"OOOOOOOH! NOT AGAIN! In the name of all that is Holy, woman, how on earth do you do this?"

The girls inquired to whom I was speaking, and then quickly informed me that Mommy was still inside the house. I thanked them for the reminder while muttering things under my breath that would have, in a just world, ignited my wife's ears into flame. I glanced down at my watch. *Late again!*

Racing around to the passenger side, I began frantically removing the great compilation of crap that she had amassed (in just a single twenty-four hour period), all the while thinking, *How in God's name could one person, in just two thirty-minute trips a day, amass so ... much...stuff?*

Why I was surprised, I am not really sure. Maybe I was hoping she had changed from the week prior, or the week prior to that, or the 572 weeks since we'd tied the knot, but that was clearly not the case.

I have asked, *Why?* before, but she just looks at me with her big brown eyes and blinks. In all honesty, I don't think she knows. She must think she needs all that *stuff*. When I ask why she doesn't bring it all in the house when she gets home, she says she has to carry the baby, and the baby is heavy, and she can't really carry much else. Being a very logical man, I ask if she has ever considered making a second trip out to the car, but then she just blinks some more. I usually just take that as a "No."

The bottom of the passenger seat was not visible ... at all. And from the floor mat to the mid-point of the back rest,

### Marital Issue #5: Poor Vehicular Hygiene

spilling over onto the coin tray and stick shift, was ... well, stuff: jackets and sweaters, a spare blouse, little pants and shirts, shoes and socks of all sizes and styles, diapers and wipes, sippy cups, juice boxes; magazines, newspapers, purses, hairbrushes, hangers; make-up including mascara, lipstick, eye shadow and blush. DVDs were strewn about, cases missing, while the portable player dangled sickly by one strap from the passenger seat headrest. The dash held Monday's mail, a package of Reese's Peanut Butter Cups — one cup consumed, one melted and reformed — and a wad of wintergreen chewing gum resting precariously on its foil wrapper just waiting for her to stop short so it could slide down the vinyl slope and hopelessly lodge itself in my defrost vent, like a white trash air freshener.

And the toys! Goodness gracious, the toys! Barbie Dolls galore — all creeds and colors, some wearing the most outrageous outfits, some scantily clad, and some not clad at all. Not to mention magnets and Legos, and hoards of stuffed animals in all shapes and sizes. And the food! All manner of snacks, opened and unopened, and even a single stick of peppered beef jerky with just a little nibble off one end. You know, the strangest part is none of us likes beef jerky, peppered or otherwise. And finally, the telltale sign that this was the handy work of my wife — two half-full Diet Pepsi cans in the cup holders, being gently warmed by the morning sun.

After uncovering the floor mat, I swiftly moved on to the always-dreaded backseat, where my two children, trained by their mother, do some of their finest work. I won't bore you with the gory details, but, oh, the food! The food!

Reaching the floor, I was confronted by enough animal crackers to start my own zoo and possibly a small traveling circus. Lions, tigers, bears, elephants, rhinos, monkeys, you name it. All I can think is that a food fight must have broken out. But how? Oh, and the Gummi bears in every color of the rainbow. Thank goodness Gummi bears have a high melting point, or my car would be one big writhing ocean of gelatin. I've done no formal research, but I'm quite certain that a post-apocalyptic world would consist of cockroaches and Gummi bears exclusively, with the former no doubt surviving on the gelatinous contents of my poor car.

What really baffles me is the sheer *quantity* of clothing and food. When I ask what possible use she could have for all the coats and sweaters, she just blinks. When I explain that we live in a very temperate climate where the risk of starving or freezing to death on her seven-mile journey to town is quite miniscule, she just blinks. When, in a serious tone, I tell her that expeditions have set off for the North Pole with fewer supplies than she takes on a fifteen-minute drive to school, she just blinks. There is no doubt Magellan circumnavigated the earth with fewer provisions, and probably at less expense. As I rapidly jettisoned flotsam into the yard, I fully expected to find some kegs of rum and couple barrels of salted pork.

Lastly, there was the trunk. What trunk, really? I will not pain you with the long laundry list of seemingly unrelated and clearly unnecessary items that occupy the trunk,

## Marital Issue #5: Poor Vehicular Hygiene

but I will say that the trunk is no longer functioning as such. It is really more of a ballast, undoubtedly intended to weigh us down and prevent our four-door Korean import from becoming airborne when exceeding speeds over 25 mph. I have not looked under the hood, nor do I intend to. In all honesty, I'm just a little afraid.

All I can figure is that in my wife's alternate universe she is like a neutron star or a black hole, with some kind of inescapable gravitational pull that sucks miscellaneous junk into orbit around her.

Well anyway, that's the situation. That's how it's been now for eleven years of semi-blissful marriage, and I just need to learn to accept it. It won't change. I've tried. Logic is a useless tack to take with my wife. She is impervious to it. A realignment of the stars would be a better focus of my energies. I do love her, though, and surely there must be some silver lining temporarily being obscured by the mounds of senseless clutter.

Come to think of it, if my family ever becomes stranded in the wilderness, I have to assume they will have enough food and drink on board to last at least one full lunar cycle, and way more than enough clothing to stave off hypothermia and frostbite. Heck, unless my count is off, the three of them may not have to wear the same outfit twice.

# The Spice of Life

Every day, to and from work, I am forced to pass this horribly controversial pornography shop that opened recently in our fine town. Considered a blight by most, that house of sin has become the source of great controversy in these parts. Why, on a daily basis, one cannot help but see our fair citizens out there exercising their right to the freedoms of speech and assembly. And until just recently, I had stayed clear of the firing lines, but I have since been drawn into this age-old battle between good and evil.

Now, as luck would have it, just one month ago, my sweet old Grammy harvested her last crate of cucumbers for the season, and she was fixing to jar up a batch of her famous spicy garlic dill pickles, a secret recipe that has been in our family since the Revolutionary War. And, boy does she make 'em spicy! In fact, there are some in our family who think those dill pickles were what killed Grandpa.

Regardless, making her special pickling brine requires a number of secret spices, most of which I can't mention, and all of which she found in short supply that day. Grammy is

## The Spice of Life

no spring chicken, but even at 92, she still gets around pretty good, so she hopped in her little car and drove off in search of seasonings. Unfortunately, en route to her favorite grocery store, she was forced to pass by that controversial new porn shop. Grammy is a private woman who doesn't read the paper much, and as luck would have it, all the anti-smut picketers had gone home for the day. So all she knew was she needed some spices and there is a value to convenience, so when she happened upon a store named Spice, she logically assumed that's what they were selling.

Now, I don't know the dumb SOB who named that smut shop "Spice" or what made him do it, but you can see how it could be more than a little misleading to a 92-year-old woman. Imagine her shock when she asked the clerk to show her where to find things for pickling. In her era, things were what they said they were, and those were not the kind of pickles to which she was referring.

So mom called me, and upon hearing this story, I went absolutely livid. I was all prepared to race down there and join the anti-smut picket lines myself, but old Grammy seemed suspiciously unphased by the whole experience. Strangely, she was looking healthier and happier than she had in years. In fact, she thanked me for my concern but told me to just forget about the whole incident.

That certainly piqued my curiosity and I feel kind of guilty about it, but I started tailing the old woman, and to my great shock, Grammy went back to that Spice shop every day for a week. It was hard to imagine, but I became fearful that my little old Grammy might be addicted to pornography. I just knew mom would be devastated. I had the need to tell *someone* of my concern, but in our family it's a no-no to cast accusations without all the facts, so I decided to do a little more investigative research first.

To begin, I set about conducting a round of interviews with all of Grammy's known associates. I started with her Bridge Club, followed by the Pink Ladies, The Red Hat Society, and the Newport Senior Center members, and each and every one of them was suspiciously tight-lipped. I got the feeling they were hiding something, but to my great frustration they were an impenetrable wall of blue hair.

I, however, have read a lot of detective novels, so I know that when it comes to interrogating suspects, there's a weak link in every chain. That said, my weak link came in the form of one Elsie May McIntyre, of 2032 Sweetbriar Lane, Seal Rock, Oregon. It seems the allure of learning the secret to Grammy's spicy garlic dill pickle brine was really more than Elsie could bear. She started providing answers to questions I hadn't even asked, and the information was making me more than a little uncomfortable.

It turns out my sweet little old Grammy made a small purchase from aisle three that day, and she was so pleased with the quality of the product, she returned a second time. And upon seeing the rejuvenating effects of those "Spices," shall we say, the girls down at the Senior Center started asking questions about the source of her healthy new glow.

Apparently word spreads quickly through the geriatric community and, according to Elsie, within the week, my 92-year-old Grammy was delivering "neck massagers," magazines

## The Spice of Life

and movies to every gray-haired old grandma in South Lincoln County. Being on a fixed income, she was forced to attach a small surcharge to cover shipping and handling, but Elsie said it was a small price to pay for serenity.

I admit it. At first I was pretty upset, but since Grandpa passed on to that great cucumber patch in the sky, why, old Grammy had seemed awful lonely and more than just a little bit tense these past few years. However, since she began frequenting the local smut shop, she's never looked more serene, and as for her appearance, well, that place is a veritable Fountain of Youth. And at the risk of sounding rude, my Grammy's neck is really none of your concern. After all, this is America, and she is an adult nearly five times over.

Friends, regarding personal love aides I have changed my position ... I mean stance ... I mean my *opinion*. We are all entitled to life, liberty, and the pursuit of happiness, and from the looks of you, you know all too well the painful pangs of sexual deprivation. Show me a citizen in defense of this boycott, and I will show you a denizen in dire need of an orgasm. Heck, old Grammy hasn't been this happy since Grandpa won the Yaquina Bay Oyster Eating contest back in the summer of '84.

# The Stowaway

It may be that my two daughters have some sort of oral deformity, but from the time they were both very young, neither one could eat anything without prodigious amounts of crumbs spilling all over themselves and the floor. It's bad enough in the house, but their mother allows them to eat in our cars as well, leaving both vehicles with a thick coating of food particles combined with liquid spills. Their weapon of choice is the cracker, but I've noticed that nothing gets consumed in its entirety, which is why it didn't really shock me last week when a large rodent scurried across the passenger floor of my car.

I tried not to panic, but there's something horribly unsettling about discovering you're not alone in your own car. Worse yet, he was big, *really big*, like a large baked potato with a tail. My hour-long commute to Lincoln City left me plenty of time to call my wife and inform her that it was all her fault, and if she wasn't always letting the kids eat in the car and she wasn't always leaving the windows down, then I wouldn't be carpooling with an enormous rodent at that present moment. She accused me of over-reacting and suggested I just leave the door open over night and allow him to escape.

As nice as that sounded in theory, I had to ask how she was so sure the creature wanted to escape and should I request that he leave me a little note to alert me when he'd gone. Something like, "Thanks for the good times, let's do it again soon."

To be perfectly honest, with the bountiful food supply, I was actually more concerned he might invite friends to the utopian biosphere. Like a vermin's version of the Garden of Eden, they could gorge themselves on a cornucopia of crumbs, sleep away the nights on my plush seats, and when nature called, relieve themselves in my cup holder. For a moment I imagined the big mouse with a tiny brown robe, sandals, and a little bitty staff, saying, "Follow me to the Promised Land, Shrews!"

Snapping back to reality, I heard my wife say, "Well, you're not going to *kill* him, are you?"

"Oh, no, of course not," I said. "I thought I'd verbally assault his little spirit and weaken his self-esteem until he just chose to leave willingly. Of course I'm going to kill him!"

"But he's just a little mouse!" she said.

"First off, he's not that little. I could probably get ticketed for not having him buckled. And second, HE'S LIVING IN MY CAR! WITH ME!"

"Well, can't you try to capture him alive then?" she asked.

"Sure," I said, "if he was the last Himalayan Snow Leopard. BUT HE'S A RODENT!"

"You're going to kill him, aren't you?" she said.

"I'll take care of it," I said.

"Well, try to make sure he doesn't suffer, okay?" she said.

"Okay, sure," I said. "Good-bye!"

Admittedly, my initial attempts at killing him were somewhat crude and poorly thought out. First I fetched a hook from my tackle box, jammed a pencil in the air vent, and then dangled some fishing line baited with a little piece of string cheese someone had conveniently left in my glove box. Hopping in the car the next morning, I was disappointed to find that "Tater" (that's what I named him), had very nimbly nibbled off all my bait and spit-polished my barbed hook. So the next night, I removed the pencil and tied the string around a thick red brick, which I had ever so delicately balanced on the edge of my dashboard. Sadly, I did not find a flattened mouse in the morning, however the brick *had* fallen and the cell phone lady gave me a great deal on a replacement phone.

Tater was up two-love, but I'm no quitter and so that very morning I marched to the grocery store and purchased a couple of ominous-looking rodent-control products called TOMCATs. Designed to look like a cat's head, the TOMCAT features a black plastic exterior, threatening saw tooth jaws, and inside the mouth a bright yellow tongue that serves as a triggering mechanism. The center of the tongue has tines on which to place your bait.

## The Stowaway

Now, I'm no dummy, so I flatly refused to pay an extra $2.99 for their special mouse-catching sauce. After all, I had unfettered access to a nearly endless supply of crumbs and bite-sized bits of cheese, and he seemed to be enjoying the crumb buffet at the Korean House of Hyundai just fine.

That night I cocked those traps, laid a little piece of extra sharp cheddar on top of those hair-trigger tongues, and went to bed with the thrill of the hunt pulsing through my blood. I awoke with the feeling that it was Christmas morning, and not wanting to ruin my surprise, I approached the car with my head turned, then *yanked* the passenger door open, thrust my head inside, and yelled, "Gotcha!"

To my great dismay, that little imp had somehow thieved my cheese right off the TOMCAT's tongue without triggering either trap. *Hair trigger my ass*, I thought. *They must not even test these damn things.*

The X-rays were negative, but my index finger did require a stitch to staunch the bleeding. The doctor said I was quite brave.

As Tater and I drove home from the hospital, I silently plotted my next move. Obviously, those traps were fully operational, so I logically deduced that the problem must lie in my choice of bait. That night I grabbed a jar of extra creamy peanut butter and dropped an irresistible dollop right in the middle of those bright yellow tongues. There was no way Tater was getting away this time. Having found a couple of long lost M&M peanuts under the seat, I tossed them on top for good measure, and went off to bed feeling confident and giddy.

## The Unnatural Aging of Cheese

I would have been happier if he'd just taken my M&Ms, or licked a little off the top, but Tater had licked those tines so clean that I could no longer tell there had ever been any peanut butter.

Every night for the next week I changed the bait menu, from peanut butter to honey to syrup to sugar, and each morning I found the same disappointing result. Like Wiley E. Coyote, I was becoming increasingly frustrated. I had really hoped to dispose of Tater with something quicker than adult-onset diabetes, but I was beginning to have my doubts. Worst of all, each passing day brought relentless mocking from friends and coworkers calling me the Great White Hunter and asking if I'd vanquished my varmint.

Try as I might, I could not convince them that this was no ordinary mouse; I was up against the Albert Einstein of the rodent world. Why, even my own children began rooting for Tater to thwart me, so it was time for Plan B, or really Plan G if you count each bait type.

Although I'd never let the cats sleep in the car before, I enlisted the services of one Sir Albert Francis Dingles III, mouse hunter extraordinaire, and his lovely partner in crime, the dainty but dangerous Tiger Lilly.

"Farewell, Tater!" I said, as the door clanged shut.

Surprisingly, sleep was difficult. I tossed and turned, dreaming of those cats tormenting that little mouse, batting him about, all while my two young daughters watched, crying, with their faces pressed to the window. Awaking in a cold sweat, I realized I could not go through with it. Jumping from bed, I pulled on my slippers and raced out to the

## The Stowaway

car, fully expecting to find Tater's tail dangling limply from a cat's mouth. Upon arrival, I found both cats looking fat and happy and sleeping soundly on the back seat.

"Oh, God!" I cried, "That poor little mouse! Am I too late?"

These days, riders always ask about the hamster wheel bolted to the passenger side floor. I tell them there's a mouse named Tater that lives under their seat, but they rarely believe me. Tater is still a little skittish around company, but he loves the kids, and if I leave an M&M peanut on the seat, he'll usually make an appearance. Admittedly, having a mouse live in your car is a bit odd, but frankly, the commute is not as lonely, and trust me when I tell you my floor is now so clean I can eat off of it.

# Sobe—So Bad!

**B**uddy had been my wife's first dog after she left home, so she took the loss particularly hard. We'd intended to wait a whole year, but after three months of watching her and our other dog, Ember, mope around, I loaded my two daughters in the car and headed down to the pound. Had I known at the time what evil lurked in my very near future, I would have gladly grabbed a goldfish and called it good.

Why didn't I just take one of the sweet lab sisters, Eliza or Do-Little? They were right *there*, but like every weak-willed father, I'm completely incapable of saying no to my daughters. He, I mean *it*, came darting out and my eldest, Cheney, said, "Awwwww, look how cute he is!" My four-year-old, Ella, was so excited she couldn't speak.

Had I just avoided eye contact that day, I'd own a good-natured lab right now. But instead, I became the not-so-proud owner of one orange Australian cattle dog, better known in my Seal Rock neighborhood as "Sobe, The Destroyer."

Admittedly, he *was* tiny and cute, and the girls had

## Sobe—So Bad!

wanted one of those yappy little Chihuahuas, so at the time, things seemed like they could have gone far worse. However, a couple of things worried me. First off, Eliza and Do-Little made no effort to steal our attention, undoubtedly viewing the threat of death as a welcome alternative to spending another day with Sobe. Secondly, the attendant kept asking if I was sure this was the dog for me.

"These dogs are *very* energetic," she said, "and they require *lots* of attention."

*Yeah, yeah, yeah,* I thought, *this ain't my first rodeo, lady. Now gimme the papers before they spot a Chihuahua.*

Last, and most disturbing, was that after setting him on the passenger seat and pulling the door shut, I felt a sudden drop in temperature. My breath began to crystallize and I could have sworn I smelled sulfur.

Just for the record, I love my children very much, but I *really* hate the pet names they pick. My youngest named Sobe after her Mother's favorite drink. He didn't look like a Sobe to me. The little runt looked more like a Dinky, so I began calling him Dinky. Unfortunately, he refused to remain dinky, and before long he was tall enough to set his front paws on the table and help himself to a person's meal. On a bright note, my kids got good about pushing in their chairs, and the younger daughter's table manners even improved. She'd routinely say, "Pwease watch my dinner, I'll be *wight* back."

One Sunday in early spring, our neighbor came over in near hysterics. Apparently Sobe had escaped and gobbled down their dinner. Quite honestly, her carrying on seemed

## The Unnatural Aging of Cheese

a bit excessive over a lost ham. Finally, I said, "Look, Mary, I've apologized, I've promised to reimburse you. Now why don't you and your kids go enjoy what's left of Easter?"

No type of corrective action seemed to help Sobe, and it wasn't long before he skipped the table, choosing to go straight to the source. Thus, all food preparation was confined to the back half of the kitchen counter and the back two burners only.

A normal dog would have been thwarted, but it turns out Sobe has a little lizard in him. Remarkably, he can extend his tongue the entire width of a kitchen counter, latch onto anything remotely edible, and pull it back to his eagerly awaiting snout. There's a region around him like a black hole, inside of which nothing escapes his pull. All matter is sucked down, its molecules ripped apart, and finally smashed into a super dense turd of singularity. It sounds unbelievable, but I actually saw him crap out a ball of light once.

The first sign of real trouble came when Sobe started digging holes. Not just any holes, but deep man-sized holes. There's one I keep expecting magma to bubble out of. The kids are excited because I've been working on a little drawbridge to go over the moat he's trenched around my home. And in what could have only been an attempt to discover the source of his being, he recently excavated my septic tank.

Not surprisingly, Sobe is a world-class escape artist and our seven-foot plank fence is no match for his evil powers of cunning. Oddly enough, he's never dug *under* the fence, instead choosing to go right straight through it. He's like one of those Jurassic Park raptors, constantly testing the perimeter for weak points. Unlike other dogs, he's got these prehistoric claws that are ideal for digging through wooden planks. I spend half my free time nailing boards over his escape routes, and I've patched my fence in so many places that it looks my yard was attacked by zombies.

When I'm not patching holes, I spend my time poop scooping. His insatiable appetite has some unpleasant residual effects. Each week, as I wander the yard armed with a garden spade and Hefty bag, I'm shocked by the recognizable remains I find embedded: Grandma's brooch, Barbie doll heads, the leg from our coffee table. One particularly fine evening I looked down and thought, *so that's where the remote went*. Based on their contents, I started assigning a cost to his poohs. I figure this fifty-dollar Shelter pup cost me about ten grand in his first—and possibly last—year of life.

That's not to say he's completely abnormal. Like all puppies, Sobe has a playful side and he lets you know by walking backward and lifting his leg like he's going to pee on your shin, but *just* before you expect a little spritz, he rests his leg down on top of your thigh. And there it stays until you play with him or chase him away. His other invitation to play involves him lifting his tail and walking backward until his butt is pressed snugly against your knee. And there he waits, frozen, as if to say, "Okay, it's your move!" Admittedly, it was pretty amusing the first time my mother-in-law came to visit, but I don't think my Boss's wife is ever coming back.

# The Unnatural Aging of Cheese

My wife recently made the mistake of leaving Sobe in the car while she ran into the bank. The metal barrier kept him out of the back seat; however he made his way down through the carpet and lifted an inch-thick plastic hatch, gaining access into the spare wheel well. Thankfully, he was unable to gnaw through the thick rubber of the tire, but he did dine on a pair of jumper cables and a survival kit. It was not a total loss because I used the remains of the jumper cable to clamp the cupboard doors back on. I have no idea what a road flare tastes like, but when I discovered the nub, I couldn't help but wish he had a taste for lit matches.

If Sobe was as smart as he thinks he is, he would have left that survival kit intact, as there is a good chance he's going to be needing it.

Surprise, surprise, Sobe has a tiny issue with chewing things. Two weeks ago I found my brand new garden hose cut into perfect six-inch sections and distributed around the yard. Fortunately, the *old* hose was reeled up on a spool and proved much more problematic. He was able to nibble only a dozen seemingly random holes in it, which makes for a pretty refreshing burst when you turn on the spigot. Last Sunday I discovered Sobe gnawed off one of the handles of my wheelbarrow. Luckily, I was able to repair it using a recently de-bristled broomstick and a plug-less extension cord.

The little devil ate both my leather gloves that I use for yard work. Oddly enough, he passed them one finger at a time. Sobe has chewed up at least half of every pair of shoes and gloves I owned. Too cheap to throw them away or

## Sobe—So Bad!

replace them, I now have a closet filled with cardboard boxes of oddball mismatches, some of which are brand new. I'm determined to get my money's worth, so despite the neighbor's funny looks, I'm still mowing the lawn in a flip-flop and a penny loafer. I know it's immature, but sometimes the staring gets to me, so I pull off an oven mitt and flip them all the bird.

Very reluctantly do we leave Sobe outside all day while we're at work. When he's not snacking on siding or dining on doorframes, he likes to drag the contents of my recycling bin out to the yard. I don't know if it's the clinking or what, but he's particularly fond of empty beer bottles. Admittedly, I'm not good about taking back my empties, so he's had as many as forty bottles scattered around the yard. No doubt my neighbors think I'm a drunk, not that Sobe doesn't give me cause.

The stress of it all caused me to over-eat, so I had to buy myself a pair of fat pants. I wore them only one day and made the mistake of leaving them on top of the washer. I'm now the proud owner of some khaki *comfortable-fit* cutoffs, which nicely complement the flip-flop/penny loafer, oven mitt/ski glove look. I've never been one to air my dirty laundry, but Sobe's taken care of that for me.

I was pretty amused the first time he dragged my wife's underwear out to the yard and tore them up. But now that I'm down to my last pair, I'm not laughing quite so hard.

Don't even talk to me about obedience school! You think I didn't think of that? After six weeks, he came in a close second ... from the bottom. He was under-performed only

# The Unnatural Aging of Cheese

by Hannibal the Cannibal, a barrel-chested Rottweiler who wore a faceguard to prevent him from eating his fellow classmates. That said, the two times they crossed paths, Hannibal was left whimpering in a puddle of his own urine. My dog is pure evil, I tell you. You don't know what I'd give for a yappy little Chihuahua right now.

# Why, You Cheating Dog, You!

**It's a little embarrassing,** but it wasn't the first time I'd been cheated on. I think it hurt more because it was the first time I'd had such an intimate relationship with the same sex. I'm over it now, and really I, more than anyone, should have known how males behave. And I should have known that when you open your heart, you always run the risk of being hurt. That said, I honestly didn't see this one coming, which made it all the more painful. We'd been together nearly three years, and you think you know them, but ... *you really don't know them.*

A week ago Wednesday, I turned into my quiet Seal Rock subdivision, started up the hill, and, that's when I saw him, in the ocean view window ... of my *neighbor's* home. An avid ornithologist, he was no doubt staring out at some passing bird.

"Why, you two-timing bastard, you!" I muttered.

Our eyes met and he tried to duck down, but he knew he was busted. In hindsight, I should have seen the signs. It all made sense then. The late nights. The poor appetite. The smell of perfume in his hair. And you know how you always start to blame yourself—Was it me? Was it something I did? The long hours at work? The lack of affection? Clearly the neighbor's home was nicer than mine, with its ocean view, and maybe the food was better too, but … was that any reason to do this to someone you supposedly loved?

Naturally, my anger and self-blame were followed by self-doubt and denial. Maybe it wasn't him in the window! Maybe I had been mistaken! My skeptical side said that those striking green eyes of his were probably one in a thousand, but still, had I really gotten a good look at him? There was only one way to be sure.

I headed home to see if he was there on my bed, splayed out, just as I'd left him that morning. Part of me didn't want to know, but part of me felt compelled to learn the truth.

I had started to convince myself it had all been just a case of mistaken identity, but then I saw what looked like his sorry white butt go scurrying across my rearview mirror. Incensed, but wanting to be absolutely sure this time, I hit the brakes, kicked the car into reverse, and started backing up to confirm my worst fears. I arrived just in time to see what appeared to be the fluffy white tail of my beloved Mr. Dingles disappearing behind a six-foot fence.

For a moment, I could see white fur and one green eye through the planks of the fence. "Mister Dingles, is that you?" I queried. And then, like white lighting, he was gone. And that's when it hit me. Why, that two-timer was trying to beat me home, and make me think that wasn't him I'd seen in the window!

## Why, You cheating Dog, You!

"Oh, no you don't," I yelled in his direction.

As everyone knows, the shortest distance between two points is a straight line, and unfortunately, since cats can take shortcuts through yards, over fences, and across rooftops, they have a distinct advantage in racing across subdivisions. Regardless, I had no intention of letting that dirty, no-good, two-timer beat me home, assuming that *was* my Mr. Dingles.

Slamming down on the accelerator, I heard the squeal of spinning tires and nearly knocked over a "children at play" sign as I peeled off down the street. Skidding around the corner of Estate Street and onto Pali Ave, I turned to see that dirty snowball skitter across Miss McKenzie's rooftop and leap onto old man Menkowintz's fence.

At that point, I appeared to have a slight edge and I felt pretty good about my chances of beating him home, but that's when I spied her out painting her fence—every neighbor's worst nightmare, that cantankerous old bat, Harrietta Grimes!

I looked on as that evil, evil woman, with her radar hearing and beady ever-watchful eyes, turned towards the sound of my approach. She had the president of our Home Owners Association on speed-dial and had already reported me for every infraction imaginable, so I had no choice but to reduce my speed.

"Daggummit!" I growled, as I watched that fluffy philanderer race into the lead.

Decelerating passed Kimo Ave, I feigned a friendly wave in Harrietta's direction and, realizing I'd lost the race,

## The Unnatural Aging of Cheese

I tried to convince myself that maybe it hadn't been Mr. Dingles after all. *Cats all look alike*, I told myself.

"Like hell that wasn't him!" I said loud enough to shock myself. The second I was out of Harrietta's line of sight, I slammed down that accelerator again and sped off. I skidded into my driveway, then burst through the front door and frantically shouted, "Has anyone seen Dingles run through here?"

My wife and daughters looked as if I was mad, but all three shook their heads, No. Turning next to the kitchen cat door, I tried to detect some signs of movement, but—nothing.

*Gosh*, I thought, *maybe it wasn't him.*

Needing to know for sure, I stormed down the hall and stopped just short of my bedroom door. This was the moment of truth. Did I really want the truth? I wasn't so sure by then, but unable to contain my cat-killing curiosity, I slowly turned the knob.

BOY, did I feel guilty. There he was, lying on the bed, sound asleep in his customary spot, just as I'd left him. How could I have been so jealous? He looked so handsome lying there, sleeping with his back to me. Hearing my approach, he lifted his sleepy little head and looked back over his shoulder in my direction. It was the look of love.

"You're such a good kitty," I said, in my coochie-coo baby voice. "Yes, Daddy loves you, Mister Dingie-wingie."

Reaching out my hand, I stroked his fluffy white belly, just the way he liked.

*Thank God!* I thought, walking over to the closet. It was

## Why, You cheating Dog, You!

merely my vivid imagination. But reaching up to unbutton my shirt, I noticed a white smudge on my hand. *Paint?*

*How*, I wondered, *had I gotten paint on myself?*

Replaying the day's events, I had no recollection of being around any paint. The only painting I'd even seen all day was that crabby cantankerous Harrietta ....

"DINGLES!" I boomed, "You cheating *dog*, you!"

He laid there as if he hadn't even heard me, but clearly the dog comment stung him a little. Despondent, I marched down the hall and flopped down in my favorite chair, unable to speak or make eye contact with my family, knowing full well that one or all of them were complicit in letting Mr. Dingles live this double life. After all, cats cannot close bedroom doors.

Five minutes later, out of the corner of my eye, I saw a white head peer around the corner. I felt his striking green eyes upon me, but I refused to return his gaze. Looking as humble as a cat is capable, he crossed the room and, reaching my feet, raised one white paw and rested it on my knee. A couple of tense moments passed, and when I didn't shoo him away, he made an incredibly presumptuous leap into my lap and nestled himself in. *How brazen of him,* I thought. *Has he no shame?* Did he really think I could ever forgive him?

Right then and there, I should have spurned his advances, but DAGNABBIT, he was *so* soft and fluffy looking. I just couldn't help myself. No doubt, people will judge me weak, but they don't understand our relationship. Maybe I am addicted to the drama, but just between you and me, Mr. Dingles and I have *great* make-up pets.

# The Finch Who Stole Christmas

**Christmas is supposed to be** such a joyous occasion, but since moving into my quaint Oregon Coast community it has been anything but. And the bane of my existence has come in the form of my neighbor to the east, one Edwin R. Finch, or "Ned" as he prefers to be called. In regards to this most recent holiday debacle, I am not normally one to point fingers, but it was clearly all Ned's fault. I may have played a small secondary role, but Ned was the instigator, and although the neighborhood children are still emotionally shaken, everyone appears to be coming to grips with what occurred.

In hindsight, the problems really started a year ago when we first moved to sleepy little Seal Rock, Oregon. It did not take me long to realize that my neighbor, Ned, was a real showboater, not to mention a nosy know-it-all, self-proclaimed jack-of-all-trades, and semi-professional landscaper. Lord knows, there is nothing I dislike more than a showboater.

Now, admittedly, lawn work is not my strong suit, nor

## The Finch Who Stole Christmas

am I terribly skilled at housework, fixing things, or cooking, but that still does not give Ned the right to humiliate me in front of my wife and children, which is exactly what he tried to do. Like any self-respecting American man, I was compelled to defend my honor and beat him at his own game. And that's really where all the trouble began.

As if his perfectly manicured lawn were not enough, Ned and his gadabout wife, Nancy, were constantly working on their homes exterior as well, for the sole purpose of making me feel inadequate. To make matters worse, they are childless and thus well rested, so they toil away tirelessly in their yard—always primping and planting and sprucing. It's quite annoying. And since I'm a hard-working man and the main breadwinner, I don't have an extra forty hours a week to keep up with those two.

That, however, did not change my feelings of inadequacy or the looks of envy and embarrassment on the faces of my wife and kids. Making matters worse was that our homes are the same size and style, so it looks like we're in some Before-and-After photo, with of course poor me being "the before."

But that's not what got me in trouble—no—I've digressed. What got me in trouble were their ridiculous lawn decorations for almost every major holiday and even several minor ones. Their garish and grandiose displays drew gawking children and passersby from miles around. Each new presentation brought a steady flow of traffic to our street, which only called more unwanted attention to the poor state of affairs on my side of the fence. It was really quite maddening, I tell you, but for the past year I have tried hard to swallow my pride and be the better man.

All the while, my elder daughter, the eight-year-old, constantly queries me on the way to school, "Daddy, why can't we decorate our house like the Finches? Daddy, why can't we have pretty lawn decorations like the Finches?" And so on and so forth she drones, all the way to town and all the way back, with occasional cheers of support from her three-year-old sister.

As a good parent, I try to explain that *"normal"* people do not spend countless hours and small fortunes decorating their yard for Cinco de Mayo and St. Patrick's Day, particularly if they were not Mexican or Irish. But, as you might imagine, this did not slow down their incessant pandering.

*Damn you, Ned!* I thought to myself.

Finally, this past Thanksgiving, unable to take it any longer, I cracked under the pressure. As I drove the family past Ned's home, I felt the mocking glare of his seven-foot inflatable turkey. That, combined with the begging coming from the mouths of my children, well, I just couldn't take it any longer.

"Hey girls," I said, "what do you say we go to Wally World tomorrow and pick up some *outside* Christmas decorations?"

"For realzies, Dad?" they asked.

"For realzies, kids," I replied.

Traditionally, I've never been an exterior decorator during the holidays, and that's just how I liked it. Oh, we're festive folk, mind you, but we're not show-offs like Ned and

## The Finch Who Stole Christmas

Nancy. We keep our decorating to the interior of the home—private—like it should be. That said, one must fight fire with fire and I knew I was up against a formidable foe.

The next day, I loaded the girls in the car and headed off to Wally World with a strict budget not to exceed $100. My Lord, I could not believe the selection! I'd never really paid attention before, but the choices are endless. And so cheap! Deals too good to pass up!

*How do those Chinese do it?* I wondered, envisioning rows and rows of them gluing little red noses on reindeer and stuffing Santa bellies. Well, I didn't want to support that shameless consumerism, so I finished grabbing my items, raced to the checkout aisle, and reluctantly paid the woman my hard-earned $175.

At the risk of sounding overly critical, Ned had been a bit predictable and unimaginative with his past Christmas decorations. He illuminated his eaves with blinking icicle lights, and in the front yard sat a silly self-inflating six-foot illuminated Tigger the Tiger wearing a Santa hat.

"Isn't that ridiculous?" I asked the girls. "What the heck does Winnie the Pooh have to do with Christmas, anyways?"

Thus we set about decorating our yard in a much more traditional manner. The girls held the ladder while I strung large-bulb multi-colored exterior lights, and then they helped me place our seven-foot illuminated Snoopy.

"Daddy?" my oldest asked. "What does Snoopy have to do with Christmas?"

"Don't be silly," I admonished her, "why, he's got his

## The Unnatural Aging of Cheese

own Christmas special. He's *way more* Christmas-y than Tigger, everyone knows that." And he was half the price of the inflatable Santa, but children don't need to be burdened with such details.

The girls placed our illuminated, wire-framed reindeer with the robotic bobbing head out by the street, while I ran our brand new 100-foot indoor/outdoor extension cord back to the house. The children were nothing short of jubilant when I plugged it in and our Snoopy instantly started to inflate and our reindeer began a bobbing. And if I do say so myself, those big bulbs looked pretty darn good along the trim of our house.

"Yeah!" my three-year-old cheered.

"Wow, our house looks way better than the Finches," my eight-year-old added.

As I checked to make sure she was correct, I reminded them that Christmas was about love and peace and the spirit of giving, and that there was no place in there for competitiveness.

The kids and I had completed our finishing touches and were waiting, expectantly, by the kitchen window for Ned to arrive home that evening. It was dark outside, but I'm pretty sure I saw Ned's eyebrows hit the roof of his spotless car when he caught sight of our home's glowing exterior, our fully inflated Snoopy, and our brilliant white reindeer bobbing in his direction, as if to say, "Yep, Ned, we won."

I know I should have been the bigger man. I know I should have been above the gloating, but for a year he had been making me look bad. And he'd been smug about it.

## The Finch Who Stole Christmas

*Let's see how* you *like humble pie, Ned,* I thought. *Want some whip cream with that?*

I knew from the time I first met Ned that the man played dirty, and the next evening when I returned from work, I was confronted by Ned's usual Christmas display, but in a clear attempt at one-upsmanship, he had also illuminated all his windows, a small maple tree, his mailbox, two large rhododendrons and a rose bush. Not to mention adding two bobbing reindeer, none of which had been part of his arsenal from the year prior. In hindsight, there were plenty of opportunities to take the proverbial high road and keep things from escalating, but my immediate reaction was, "All right then, Ned. If that's how you want it. GAME ON!"

As any responsible parent would have done, I feigned illness the next day, picked the girls up early from school, and we headed straight to Wally's where we grabbed another 150-foot extension cord, eight strands of blinking icicle lights, and two more illuminated reindeer, bringing our herd to three. Last but not least, I also purchased the new centerpiece of our display, an illuminated, eight-foot self-inflating Santa. In an effort to show my children the benefits of hard work and good sportsmanship, we raced home, installed the decorations, and then went to the kitchen window to await Ned's arrival. Man-o-man did he looked surprised. Shocked is more like it. Defeated is actually a more apt description. Now, I'm no mind reader, but old Ned looked like he realized he'd bitten off a little more inflatable turkey than he could chew.

# The Unnatural Aging of Cheese

Sadly, my enjoyment was short-lived, because the following day Ned struck back with some pulsating snowflake eave-hangers, a six-foot inflatable Frosty in a tree, and two more wire reindeer, bringing his herd to four. Most of his parries were tired and predictable, but I must say the tree-mounted snowman was a nice touch. However, I refused to be bested.

The next day I counter-attacked with some blinking snowflake driveway liners, lighted rope to line our walkway, and two more reindeer, bringing our total herd to five. Not to be outdone, that darn-blasted Ned added an inflatable female companion for his snowman, a four-foot snow globe with self-stirring snow, and two more reindeer for a total of six. *You're an evil, evil man, Ned,* I thought. *You and your festive inflatables and devilishly illuminated reindeer.*

Finally, on Christmas Eve day, as I prepared to head back to Wally World, my wife finished balancing our checkbook and discovered that I'd purchased 750 feet of extension cord in just twenty-five days. She—I mean I—decided enough was enough, and that we could scarcely afford to continue waging this war. She ordered—I mean requested—that I end it, once and for all. At that point, recognizing that things had spiraled horribly out of control, I agreed to cease and desist, right after I grabbed the kids and snuck off to Wally's one last time.

I did it only for the children. After all, it's not good for them to think their father is a quitter. And every good battle needs to end with a coup de grace, so I returned home with an enormous inflatable Santa riding in a sleigh with a giant

## The Finch Who Stole Christmas

bag of toys. And five more reindeer, just to complete our set.

"Take that, Ned," I said.

Then, to maximize the impactfulness, we tethered the sleigh and all nine reindeer together and I mounted them on the top of my roof. We even jerry-rigged a red bulb for the tip of the lead reindeer's nose. At that point, standing in the street to admire our handy work, the children and I were just giddy with delight. Sensing that the end was near, we ran back inside to await Ned's return. *Well, Ned,* I thought, *That's a wrap, no pun intended.*

To my great surprise, Ned actually came over and complimented me and the kids on our wonderful Christmas display. My wife thought him sincere, but I found it disingenuous at best. Then, in an underhanded, Trojan Horse maneuver that only Ned would have the audacity to try, he actually suggested I deflate my entire display before the big windstorm hit that night.

I was about to ask, "What windstorm?" when I realized what he was up to.

"Come on, Ned!" I said, "You'll have to do better than that!"

"Suit yourself," he suspiciously replied.

I must admit it was a nice touch when Ned went home and deflated his own display, but I wasn't about to fall for it. Victory is mine! I thought.

Surprisingly, about eight o'clock that night, the wind *did* start to pick up a bit. My wife suggested maybe Ned was just being helpful.

## The Unnatural Aging of Cheese

"Nonsense!" I cried. "It's just a light breeze! Just coincidence, at best."

Little did she know that there was nothing to worry about because I'd safely secured each individual reindeer to the roof using double knots and the finest twine Wally's had for sale.

Shockingly, about nine o'clock, we encountered sustained winds of 50 mph. My wife gave me a concerned look. In my defense, before we moved to the Oregon Coast, no one had ever told me about 100 mph storms.

Just before ten o'clock that night we heard an unusual flapping that concerned even me. As I ran outside, I was alarmed to see that Santa and his sleigh had detached from the roof and were being lifted several feet up with each gust of wind. Racing into the garage, I grabbed my ladder and had just rambled over the gutter when I heard the first reindeer—I believe it was Blitzen—give way under the stress.

*Uh-oh*, I thought. A moment later, I heard the noise again, followed shortly thereafter by seven similar and subsequent ripping sounds.

Before there was time to do *anything*, Santa lifted off like a hot air balloon and sailed into the night sky. Disturbingly, he was flying upside down and backward due to the weight of the reindeer. And worst of all, as he flew away, he remained illuminated thanks to 300 feet of indoor/outdoor extension cord. As shocking as the whole scene was, I found myself muttering, "On Dasher, on Dancer, on Prancer and Vixon, on Comet and Cupid, and Donner, and Blitzen."

And then the whole unholy abomination slammed into

## The Finch Who Stole Christmas

Old Lady Olmstead's house, blinked out, and collapsed to the ground in a tangled heap of bent wire and nylon.

*Oops!* I thought to myself.

Unfortunately, there were a number of young children on our street who witnessed the whole scene. Despite their parents' assurances that Santa would be just fine, they were reportedly inconsolable. They are currently receiving therapy, but it may be a while before it's clear whether any permanent damage was done. Kids are resilient, so I'm staying positive.

Needless to say, I definitely learned my lesson. No more inflatables for me. I've just built a much sturdier sled out of an old armoire, an easy boy recliner, and a pair of cross-country skis I picked up at a yard sale. Just let ol' Ned try to top me this year!

Speaking of whom, if it hadn't been for Ned and that childish competitive streak of his, then the Christmas Eve fiasco never would have happened. Why, he should be ashamed of himself.

# If I Could Be Like Mike

What I wouldn't give to go back 100,000 years and get my hands on that first overachieving Neanderthal who came strutting back to his cave dragging a Saber-toothed tiger in each hand. I would promptly relieve him of his club and commence to decorating his thick skull with lumps—one for each of my fellow underachievers who have suffered through the ages.

That thickheaded fool and his decedents—King Tut, Peter the Great, Ben Franklin and the like—set a precedent to which no underachieving adolescent like myself could ever live up to. And then there is the latest in their abhorrent line, the bane of my own existence, one Michael Brian Hoos, overachiever extraordinaire.

No doubt the disappointed fathers of all those empty-handed Neanderthals held up Mr. Two-Tigers as a shining example of how they wanted their sons to be, which is exactly what my father did to me with the aforementioned Mr. Hoos. Back when I was a kid, every time I had Dad settled into a healthy, unquestioning acceptance of my mediocrity,

## If I Could Be Like Mike

why, that idiot Hoos would run off and get himself in the paper for one wonderful achievement or another. And then there was the inevitable, "Well, why can't you be more like Mike?"

"Because I, the fruit of your loins, am delightfully average," I'd say. "Besides, if I did all those things Mike is doing, like feeding the homeless after school and teaching orphans how to read on weekends, then I'd have no time to get in any trouble, and that wouldn't be fair for you, Father, who, in my humble opinion, needs practice on your parenting skills."

Sadly, no gesture of appreciation ever ensued.

Thus, my final two years of high school—after I'd been expelled from a $15,000 a year boarding school and had the misfortune of making Mr. Hoos' acquaintance—were spent with my father unfairly comparing me to that obnoxious, overachieving do-gooder.

"Oh, look," he'd say, his face buried in the local paper, "Mike made honor roll again. Why don't you ever get straight A's, Steve?"

"I don't know, Dad," I'd say, "I guess I like a little variety on my report card."

"Oh, look," he'd say, "Mike made all-conference in football." Then, "Oh look, Mike saved a poodle from a burning tree." Then, "Oh look, Mike was elected president of the debate club. Why can't you be president of the debate club, Steve?"

"I don't know, Dad," I'd say, "is that a rhetorical question? Look at it this way," I'd say, "without me, there'd be no baseline by which to measure how great Mike is, so in actuality, your son is the standard by which they measure greatness around here, and that's something you can really be proud of, Dad."

My verbal parry appeared to puzzle him.

Oh, did I mention that Mike was one of my closest friends? Which only served to make matters worse.

When my father wasn't reading about Mike in the newspaper, or running into his parents in the grocery store, he would get firsthand accounts of Mike's stupendous accomplishments and frighteningly well-thought out future. Dad would then invariably ask me what *my* plans were for the future and I'd say, "Gosh, I don't know, Father. I thought maybe I'd have a sandwich around lunch time."

Our senior year, when I thought things could not get any worse, Mike went and got a senator to recommend him for admission to the highly prestigious West Point Military Academy.

*Oh, you dummy*, I thought. *Now you've gone and done it.*

I knew what was coming next, and sure enough, the moment the news hit the papers, my father said, "Oh, look, Mike got appointed to West Point! That's probably going to save his parents $200,000 in tuition. Why can't you get a scholarship and save me some money?" he asked.

"Well," I said, "even if I pull down straight A's this semester, which I wouldn't recommend you bet the house on, then it still wouldn't do much to pull up my D+ average, for which they dole out scholarships somewhat sparingly. But look at it this way, Dad, I probably saved you $150

## If I Could Be Like Mike

grand by not being smart enough to get into an Ivy League school." Sadly, he didn't appear to recognize any value in that argument.

Once I'd grown up, moved to the West Coast, and had children of my own, I thought my feelings of inadequacy were far behind me. But, not long after I turned forty, there came that awful call again.

"Hey, did you hear about Mike getting promoted to Lieutenant Colonel?" my father's voice said.

I know it shouldn't have bothered me, and I should have been happy for my friend, but the reverence in my father's voice was too much for me to bear. And the ensuing question about why I couldn't have had a distinguished career like that was only worsened by the fact that I'd spent many years mired in middle management, and the highest military rank I'd ever held was a takeout order of General Tso's Chicken.

After years of keeping the bar of parental expectations nice and low, something I could easily hop over, Hoos had gone and messed things up for me again. And though this final indignity was more than I could stand, I had no intentions of working any harder, so I decided to employ a new tack. Like I always say, "if you can't beat them, try to get them to slow down so it looks like you lost by less." Thus, I chose to call Lieutenant Colonel Hoos and share a bit of wisdom that a wise, old black man had once imparted to me.

Many, *many* years ago, Ol' Cholly had been worried that my fast pace of furniture removal was going to make the

## The Unnatural Aging of Cheese

other fellas look bad, and quite possibly end our day early, so he graciously enlightened me—as I now planned to do to Hoos. After a couple rings he picked up and I said, "Now just *slow down*, little brother ... we gettin' paid by the *hour*—not by the *piece*."

# About the Author

**STEVE CHRISMAN** is a graduate of Southern Oregon University (barely), and he lives, blissfully, in the tiny town of Seal Rock, Oregon, with his incredibly tolerant wife Shannon, two daughters, two dogs and two cats.

He was born in Laguna Beach, California, but raised in a suburb of Philadelphia. He graduated from Manasquan High School (barely), on the Jersey Shore, and lived in the states of Washington and Alaska before moving to Oregon.

When Steve is not choking on burnt food or waiting for his daughters to get out of the bathroom, he can be found walking his dogs on the miles of beautiful and nearly uninhabited beaches near his home.

Sadly, Thurston P. Snuffington III (aka Buddy) died in 2008, but his memory lives on in Sobe the Destroyer.